pacific
knits

by Alexa Ludeman
& Emily Wessel

Tin Can Knits
Vancouver, CANADA

contents

sitka spruce
torrent

hipster
lions gate

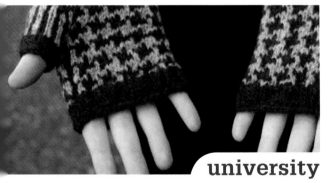

university
main street

mukluks

low tide   kits kerchief

antler   tofino surfer

north shore   false creek

campfire   rosebud

urban hiker   sea to sky

pacific knits

irrisistible earthy knits   *by Alexa Ludeman and Emily Wessel*

The Pacific Coast of Canada is a very special place, beloved by those who live here. We live in cities, but these cities are situated in majestic landscapes. Mountains to one side, the ocean on the other, and verdant forests in between - look in any direction and you see beauty.

Landscape and climate have created a unique west-coast lifestyle. We challenge you to try the Vancouver Trifecta: kayak, hike, and snowboard all in the same day... clad in exquisite knits, of course!

While we are city dwellers, hints of our pioneering past remain. The coast has only recently been home to European settlers and modern conveniences. Here the great-granddaughters of frontierswomen wear wool (under their goretex) and are praised for their skills at chopping wood and starting fires.

Amazing landscape, our love of playing in the outdoors, and a laid-back urban vibe inspired this collection of knits. Our surroundings are both rustic and urban, wild and pretty, and the designs reflect this - capturing the serene, the playful, and the rugged.

Curl up next to your wood stove, grab some local hand-dyed yarn, and get to work creating something beautiful for yourself or your loved ones! All the designs are sized for the whole family, because we know your adorable little man wants to dress just like your sexy old man!

From hipster to housewife, beginner to expert, we have crafted this collection for you!

With all our love ❤

Emily & Alexa

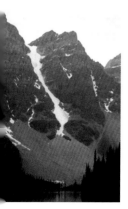

This book is intended as a pattern collection, not a technical reference. The advanced techniques used in our patterns are briefly described here.

For links to step-by-step tutorials covering these techniques in depth, visit **www.tincanknits.com**

basic stitch patterns you should know:
stockinette stitch: knit RS rows, purl WS rows
garter stitch: knit all rows
seed stitch: (k1,p1), following rows knit the purls and purl the knits
ribbing: 1x1 is (k1,p1) 2x2 is (k2,p2) twisted rib is (k1-tbl, p1), following rows knit the knits and purl the purls.

blocking:
blocking consists of washing your knit and letting it dry so the stitches relax into their final form. Blocking radically improves most knitted projects. For fair-isle and lace projects it is crucial. To block lace, allow it to soak until fully saturated, squeeze out as much water as possible in a towel, then pull it tightly and pin it into place. Leave the piece until completely dry, then unpin and 'voila' the lace pattern is revealed.

cables & twisted stitches:
cables and twisted stitches are methods of knitting stitches out of regular order to create twists in the fabric. To work cables, you use a cable needle to put a number of stitches on hold, while you knit stitches further along the row. Then you knit the earlier stitches, and the swap creates a twist in the fabric itself. Brilliant and dead easy! Try it!

casting on and binding off:
There are methods for casting on and binding off. To achieve an excellent finished result you must pay additional attention at the CO and BO points. If the first method you try doesn't look right, try a different method or use different needles to alter the tension.

charts:
chart are read from right to left, and from bottom (row 1) to top. Each square represents a stitch (as indicated by the key). Repeats are indicated by heavy lines, and are worked as many times as will fit in each row. While some charts illustrate every row, others illustrate only RS or odd numbered rows, with the WS or even numbered rows described by text instructions. Always read chart notes and key carefully before you start.

fair-isle / stranded knitting:
stranded knitting uses two or more colours of yarn at a time to create multicoloured patterns. You knit a number of sts with one colour, then switch to the other colour, and knit a few more. The yarn not currently in use is carried loosely behind the work, creating 'floats'. It is important to relax and allow these floats to be very loose, so the fabric maintains elasticity and does not pull in too much. Another consideration when working stranded patterns is 'yarn dominance'. Essentially, the yarn that is brought up from underneath the other is more dominant and creates slightly larger and more 'dominant' stitches. When working a pattern, consider which part you want to 'pop' more, and carry that yarn on the bottom consistently.

techniques

kitchener stitch: Kitchener stitch, also known as 'grafting' or 'weaving' is a seamless method to join stitches. It essentially forms a new row in between two rows of live stitches. With a darning needle and yarn weave back and forth across the gap, maintaining the looping patter of the knitted fabric.

increasing and decreasing: Decreases gather two or more stitches from the previous row into 1 stitch, 'decreasing' the stitch count. And increases add to the stitch count. When worked in the same place every row, increases have a tendency to 'slant' one way or the other. For example k2tog leans to the right, and ssk to the left. But frankly, the method you use to increase and decrease is NOT THAT IMPORTANT. So you can use the method we suggest, or your own favorite way!

increase / decrease x stitches, evenly spaced: OK, so you have seen this instruction, and you probably hate us now. But we would like to humbly suggest you untwist your skivvies, and learn a skill or two.

Take it slowly. You have 150 sts on the needles. You are meant to increase 20 sts, evenly spaced. 150 / 20 is 7.5 . So simply increase 1 stitch after 7 sts (k7,m1) a total of 20 times, then knit whatever sts remain without increasing.

OR the converse (a little more complicated...) You have 150 sts, and are instructed to dec 20 sts, evenly spaced. so 150 / 20 = 7.5. So 7 is the largest WHOLE number that goes into 150. So you can work (k2tog, k5) (that's 7 stitches) 20 times, then knit the remaning stitches even to end of round.

If you have 200 sts, and you're told to decrease 7, evenly spaced, well, essentially... WHO CARES where you put them. (Knit a bunch, k2tog) seven times. It's EASY. What's the bottom line here, ladies and gentlemen? Repeat it with me now... It's EASY. Git er done!

lace: lace is formed by a series of artfully arranged holes. These holes are created by yarn-over increases, and these increases are balanced by corresponding decreases. Essentially, if learn how to make a yarn-over stitch and know how to work decreases like k2tog and ssk, you can work lace! It's great; we think you should try it!

picking up stitches: with RS facing, insert needle between sts (or rows), yarn over with working yarn on WS, and pull a loop through knitted fabric to RS (*one st picked up*). Repeat until desired sts have been picked up. *(this technique is referred to as 'pick up and knit' in some patterns)*

provisional cast on (crochet chain method): Using waste yarn, crochet a chain a few sts longer than you plan to cast on. With knitting needles and working yarn, insert needle under back bump of last crochet chain stitch. Yarn over and pull up a stitch. Continue along crochet chain, creating as many sts as required. To 'unpick' the provisional cast on, unfasten the end and it will 'unzip', leaving live sts ready to be worked.

put stitches on hold: Instead of binding off, thread a piece of waste yarn through the live stitches, so they don't unravel, and then remove the needles. You may alternately choose to use a stitch holder, but we generally suggest using waste yarn, as it is pliable and does not pull on the stitches.

short row shaping: To work short rows, you knit part of the way through a row, then stop and turn around before the end. Work as pattern specifies to the point where it says 'wrap and turn' or 'w&t'. To 'wrap and turn', knit the last st indicated, then slip the next st purlwise from LH needle to RH needle, then bring the yarn from back to front, then slip the stitch back to LH needle, and pass the yarn from front back to the back of work. The yarn will now 'wrap' around the base of this unworked stitch. Turn the work, and work in the opposite direction per the pattern. When the pattern says 'pick up wraps', this means that when you come to a wrapped stitch, pick up the wrap and work the wrap and the stitch together (using either a k2tog or p2tog).

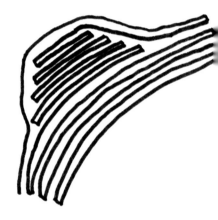

substituting yarns: Well, we have knit these projects in the most beatiful yarns known to man, don't you want to do the same? We recommend wool and wool blends. Wool is very forgiving (stretchy), can be blocked to adjust size, and makes for beautiful finished projects. For easy care we suggest machine-washable wools. Hand-dyed sock yarns are particularly well-suited to projects intended for babies; if held double a sock yarn can substitute for a worsted / aran weight yarn. So much time and love goes into your knits, so spend the money on quality materials for exquisite results.

abbreviations

abbreviations:

c#b	**cable # back** - slip #/2 sts to cn, hold in back of work, knit #/2 sts from LH needle, knit #/2 sts from cn.
c#f	**cable # front** - slip #/2 sts to cn, hold in front of work, knit #/2 sts from LH needle, knit #/2 sts from cn.
CC	contrast colour
cn	cable needle
CO	cast on
dec	decrease(d)
dpns	double pointed needles
inc	increase(d)
k	knit
k2tog	knit two stitches together
k3tog	knit three stitches together
kf&b	knit into the front and back of the same stitch
kll	knit left loop - knit into back loop of st below next st
krl	knit right loop - use LH needle to pick up stitch below stitch just knitted, then knit into it
k-tbl	knit through back loop of stitch
L	left
LH	left-hand
m1	make one stitch (any method)
m1R	make one right - use LH needle to lift bar between sts from front, knit into back of loop.
m1L	make one left - use RH needle to lift bar between sts from back, knit into front of loop
MC	main colour
mm	millimeters
mo	months (as in 0-6 mo)
N1(2,3)	needle 1(2,3) *(double pointed needles)*

p	purl
p2tog	purl two stitches together
p3tog	purl three stitches together
PM	place marker
p-tbl	purl through back loop
rep	repeat
req'd	required
rnd	round
RS	right side of the work
RH	right hand
R	right
sl1	slip one stitch *(purlwise unless specified)*
sl1-k2tog-psso	slip 1 knitwise, knit two together, pass slipped stitch over
ssk	slip 2 sts knitwise, knit 2 sl sts together through back loops
sssk	slip 3 sts knitwise, knit 3 together through back loops
st.st.	stockinette stitch
st(s)	stitch(es)
tbl	through back loop(s) of stitch(es)
tog	together (as in k2tog, p2tog, etc.)
yds	yards
yo	yarn over (yarn forward/yfwd)
yrs	years
WS	wrong side of the work

work as established or 'as set' or 'in pattern' continue in pattern; knit the knit sts and purl the purl sts from previous row. In lace, you typically knit the yo sts (or purl on the WS) and purl the p2togs

w&t	wrap and turn (for short rows)

creating beloved hand knits:

There are many ways to skin a cat, and many methods for wrapping your beloved babes in hand-knits! If you are intending to face the sweater curse head-on, I wish you the best of luck and hope you will consider the following tips and suggestions.

An ill-fitting sweater is **probably** not cause for a dumping... but lets not take the chance! The best way to knit a sweater that will work for the wearer is to base it upon one that you / he / she already likes. Lay the sweater flat on the floor and measure:

1. Chest / Bust
2. Sleeve length (underarm to cuff)
3. Body length from underarm to hem

Armed with these critical dimensions, you can choose the correct size from the pattern options, and determine how to adjust arm and body lengths (if at all). For most situations, this is all that you will need to change. If you are inclined to stray a bit further off the well-defined path... well I hope to meet you out in the woods!

*I don't care if you knit a gauge swatch... because I don't care if your sweater fits. But **you** should! Many knitters have met desperate and depressing ends due to the TERRIBLE decision to skip the swatch. I hope it won't happen to you...*

seamless knits: All of the knits in this collection are virtually seamless. All but one are knit from the bottom up, in the round where possible. Sleeves are knit first, in the round. Then the body is knit in the round (for a pullover) or in rows (for a cardigan) all the way up to the underarm. To complete the garment, you work the yoke all at once on a longish circular needle, working the front, sleeve, back, sleeve, then the front again. The yoke is worked in rounds for a pullover, and in rows for a cardigan. Upon arrival at the neckline, the sweaters are finished by various methods.

We design our patterns this way because it is simple, non-fussy, and that is how we like to knit them!

Because the garments are knit from the bottom up, if you need to make adjustments to the length of body or arms, you must do it before you join all the pieces together for the yoke.

FAV sweater

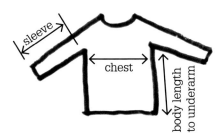

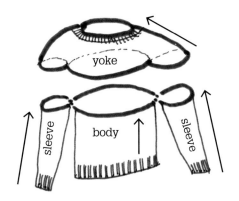

A seamless sweater is a series of tubes:

Three tubes: sleeve, body, sleeve join to become one BIG tube: yoke which decreases to a little head-sized tube at the collar.
Voila it's magic... a sweater!

sweaters

... if you really loved me, you would knit me a sweater...

gorilla arms? sleeve and body length given in our patterns act as your guide, but for a perfectly customized knit, these are very simple places to adjust; simply knit longer in the body or in the arms before joinning the garment at the yoke.

shorter sleeves? A couple of the designs here would look cute with 3/4 length or elbow-length sleeves. It's simple. Take a look at the number of stitches cast on, and the number of stitches you work to (total at underarms), and just cast on a number somewhere in the middle. Then follow the pattern to increase to the upper arm total, and work to your desired length.

curvilicious? We designed these patterns without waist shaping, because we wanted them to be simple and unisex. We think they look pretty fabulous without shaping, but you may choose to add it in. The goal is to pinch the stitch count in at the waist, so decrease leading up to the waist point, and then increase after the waist back to the bust. You can play it by ear, or onsult the experts: there are entire reference books focused to the many ways to shape your knits to better suit your body.

north shore

fair-isle head turner *by Alexa Ludeman and Emily Wessel*

Ocean, trees, mountains: these are the basic building blocks of the Pacific Coast. Vancouver's North Shore has all of the above. You can kayak along sandy beaches, hike through steeply wooded slopes, and to ski tour over the glaciers and icefields of the Coast Mountains. This fair-isle pattern is an ode to our beloved west-coast landscape!

sizing: The pattern includes 7 child and 8 adult sizes:
0-6 mo (6-12 mo, 1-2 yrs, 2-4 yrs, 4-6 yrs, 6-8 yrs, 8-10 yrs,
Adult XS, S, M, L, XL, XXL, 3XL, 4XL)

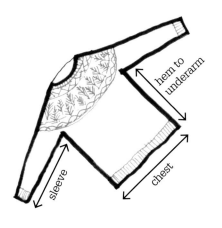

Size	Chest	Sleeve	Hem to Underarm	Yardage MC	CC 1-4
0-6 mo	18"	7.5"	6"	300	40 ea
6-12 mo	19"	8"	5.5"	330	40 ea
1-2 yrs	20"	9"	7.0"	360	40 ea
2-4 yrs	22"	10.5"	8"	400	50 ea
4-6 yrs	24"	12"	10"	500	50 ea
6-8 yrs	26"	14"	13"	600	50 ea
8-10 yrs	28"	16"	15"	750	50 ea
Adult XS	31"	18"	15"	900	60 ea
S	35"	19"	16"	1100	60 ea
M	39"	19"	17"	1200	60 ea
L	43"	20"	18"	1300	60 ea
XL	47"	20"	19"	1400	70 ea
XXL	51"	21"	19.5"	1500	70 ea
3XL	55"	21"	20"	1600	70 ea
4XL	59"	21"	20"	1700	70 ea

materials:

Yarn: DK weight yarn in 5 colours - **refer to table for yardage** pullover requires one MC and CC1, CC2, CC4, CC4 (*sample shown in Tanis Fiber Arts Yellow Label DK in 'teal', 'tidal', 'natural', 'charcoal' and 'lemongrass'*)

Gauge: 22 sts / 4" in stockinette stitch using larger needles

Needles: US #4 / 3.5mm and US #6 (4.0mm); *(or as req'd to meet gauge)* circular and double pointed needles in each size (16" circular for small sizes, 24"-32" for larger sizes)

Notions: stitch markers, darning needle

pattern: This pullover has simple construction. Body and sleeves are knit in the round to the underarm then joined onto 1 needle for the yoke, which is shaped by a series of decrease rows between fair-isle patterns.

sleeves: Using MC and smaller needles CO 32 (32,32,36,36,40,40,**44,48,48,52,52,56,60,64**) sts, PM and join for working in the round.

Work in 2x2 rib (k2,p2 around) for 1.5 (1.5, 1.5, 2, 2, 2, 2, **2, 2, 2.5, 2.5, 2.5, 2.5, 2.5, 2.5**) inches. Change to larger needles and knit 1 round.

Increase round: k1, m1, knit to last st, m1, k1
Knit 5 rounds.

Repeat these 6 rounds until there are 38 (40,42, 48,56,60,64,**68,72,74,80,84,88,94,104**) sts.

Work in stockinette until sleeve measures 7.5 (8, 9, 10.5, 12, 14, 16, **18, 19, 19, 20, 20, 21, 21, 21**) inches *(or desired length)*.

Place the first and last 3 (3,3,3,4,4,4,**4,4,4,5,5,5,6, 6**) sts of the round on hold for underarm, and the remaining sts on hold separately. Work second sleeve the same as first.

body: Using MC and smaller needles CO 100 (104,112,120,132,144,152,**172,192,216,236,260, 280,300,324**) sts. PM and join for working in the round.

Work in 2x2 rib for 1.5 (1.5, 1.5, 2, 2, 2, 2, **2, 2, 2.5, 2.5, 2.5, 2.5, 2.5, 2.5**) inches.

Change to larger needles and work in stockinette stitch until body measures 6 (6.5, 7, 8, 10, 13, 15, **15, 16, 17, 18, 19, 19.5, 20, 20**) inches *(or desired length)*.

join sleeves and body for yoke:
PM, then place the next 6 (6,6,6,8,8,8,**8,8,8,10, 10,10,12,12**) body sts on hold (L underarm). Knit left sleeve sts (except underarm sts).

Knit 44 (46,50,54,58,64,68,**78,88,100,108,120, 130,138,150**) body sts, place next 6 (6,6,6,8,8,8,**8, 8,8,10,10,10,12,12**) body sts on hold (R underarm). Knit across right sleeve as at left, then knit to end of body sts. [152 (160,172,192, 212,232,248,**276,304,332,356,388,416,440,484**) sts.] Start of round is behind left shoulder.

Knit 1 (1,1,2,2,3,3,**5,7,7,7,7,7,7,7**) rounds.

Next Round: decrease 2 (0,2,12,12,2,18,**16,4, 22,26,18,36,40,44**) sts evenly spaced.
[150 (160,170,180,200,230,230,**260,300,310,330, 370,380,400,440**) sts]

The start of round is behind the L shoulder.

fair-isle yoke: refer to charts A, B and C.
If you tend to work at a tighter gauge when knitting colourwork, you may want to switch to a larger needle size.

work chart A (waves): in MC, CC1 and CC2

Next Round (decrease) (work in MC)

Child Sizes: decrease 0 (0,10,10,10,10,10) sts, evenly spaced

Adult XS to XXL:
[k2tog, k**11(13,13,14,16,17**)] 20 times, knit to end

Adult 3XL and 4XL: [k2tog, k**11(12**)] 30 times, knit to end

[150 (160,160,170,190,220,220,**240,280,290,310, 350,360,370,410**) sts]

work chart B: trees in CC3 and CC4.
Child sizes 0-6mo to 1-2 yrs omit rounds 1-7 of chart B, working only rounds 8-17.

Chart repeat decreases from 10 sts to 7 sts.
[105 (112,112,119,133,154,154,**168,196,203,217, 245,252,259,287**) sts]

Next Round: in CC3, decrease 5 (2,2,9,3,4,4, **18,16,3,17,5,2,9,7**) sts, evenly spaced.

Next Round (Adult sizes S to 4XL only):
in CC3, [k2tog, k3(4,2,2,4,3,3,3)] around

[100 (110,110,110,130,150,150,**150,150,150,150, 200,200,200,210**) sts]

work chart C: mountains in CC 1,2,3,

Switch to MC, and work as follows:

0-6 mo to 2-4 yrs: (k2tog, k3) around

4-6 yrs: (k2tog, k3) around. Then knit one more round, decreasing 8 sts evenly spaced.

6-8, 8-10 yrs, XS: (k2tog, k1) around

S, M, L: (k2tog, k3) around. Then knit 1 more round, decreasing 16(12,12) sts, evenly spaced.

XL, XXL, 3XL: (k2tog, k1) to last 2 sts, k2. Then knit 1 more round, decreasing 22 (18,18) sts.

4XL: (k2tog, k1) around. Then knit 1 more round, decreasing 20 sts, evenly spaced.

CHILD SIZE CHARTS

chart C : mountains

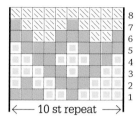

←— 10 st repeat —→

ADULT SIZE CHARTS

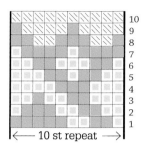

←— 10 st repeat —→

chart B : trees

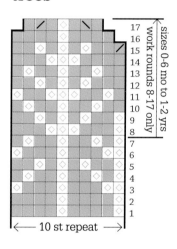

sizes 0-6 mo to 1-2 yrs work rounds 8-17 only

←— 10 st repeat —→

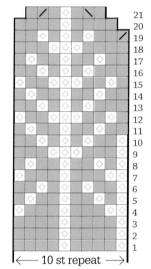

←— 10 st repeat —→

chart A : waves

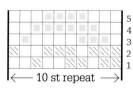

←— 10 st repeat —→

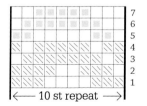

←— 10 st repeat —→

Chart Notes:

Charts are read from R to L. As knitting is in the round, all rows are RS rows, and all sts are knit. For child sizes use LH charts, for adult sizes use RH charts. Refer to text instructions for decrease rows worked between charts. Sizes 0-6mo, 6-12mo, and 1-2 yrs: when working chart B, work only rows 8 to 17, omitting rows 1-7.

short row shaping: you may choose to work a series of short rows at the back of neck for a more comfortable fit.

Throughout the yoke, the start of round marker has been located behind the left shoulder. To work short rows, you must mark approximate shoulder points. Knit 8 to 11 sts, PM for left shoulder, k40(44,44,44,48,50,50,**50,52,54,54, 56,58,58,60**), PM for right shoulder. Stop, lay out the sweater, and assess if the marker seem to be at approximately the correct locations (this is an inexact science, since the yoke is circular). If not, move the markers until they seem to be at each shoulder, with equal sts between them. The short rows are worked across the back.

Work short rows:

knit to 8 sts past left shoulder marker, w&t
purl (across the back) to 8 sts past right shoulder marker, w&t
knit to 10 sts before wrapped st, w&t
purl to 10 sts before wrapped st, w&t

Repeat previous 2 short rows an additional 0 (0,0,0,0,0,0,**1,1,1,1,2,2,2,2**) times.

collar: Switch to smaller needles, and work in 2x2 ribbing for 6 (6, 6, 7, 7, 7, 7, **7, 7, 11, 11, 11, 11, 11, 11**) rounds. Bind off loosely.

finishing: Graft underarm sts, sew up the small holes either end, and weave in all ends. Block your sweater and wear with pride!

irresistible earthy knits by Alexa Ludeman and Emily Wessel

sitka spruce

boldly textured hat and mitts 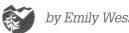 *by Emily Wessel*

The temperate rainforests of the Pacific Northwest are home to many species of evergreen, including the sitka spruce. Walking here you can hug the big trees, smell the moss and damp earth, and listen as the ancient trees whisper to one another. The light that filters down through the canopy far above is green and magical.

The twisted stitch pattern that adorns the hat and mittens is elegant, geometrical and unisex. The pattern includes instructions for a snug beanie and a slouchier beret style hat.

sizing:

Mittens: Adult S (M, L)
Finished palm measurement: 7 (7.75, 8.5) inches
Finished hand height: 6.5 (7.5, 8.5) inches

*For Child size (finished palm 5.5 inches, hand height 6 inches)
work adult small instructions in DK weight yarn at 22sts/4 inches*

Hat: Pattern written for beanie (beret) styles of hat
Hat fits adult head 20-22 inches in circumference
Blocking can be used after-the-fact to adjust size

For small (large) child sizes, work beanie (beret) instructions in DK weight yarn at 22 sts / 4 inches. Fits head circumference 16 (18) inches

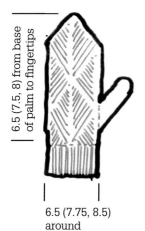

6.5 (7.5, 8) from base of palm to fingertips

6.5 (7.75, 8.5)
around

materials:

Yarn: worsted / aran weight yarn
Hat: 150 (180) yds
Mittens: 130 (140, 160) yds
(sample shown in Malabrigo Worsted in 'lettuce')

Gauge: 18 sts / 4" in stockinette stitch *(using larger needles)*

Needles: US #7 / 4.5mm and US #8 / 5.0mm *(or as req'd to meet gauge);* 20" circular needle and double pointed needles

Notions: stitch markers, darning needle

sitka spruce hat:
The hat is knit in the round from brim to crown.

Using smaller needles CO 96 sts. Join for working in the round and begin twisted ribbing: (k1-tbl, p1) around. Work a total of 10 rounds in ribbing.

For beret style only work increase round:
[k1, p1, k1, p1, m1, k1, m1, p1, m1, k1, m1, p1, k1, p1, k1, p1] around [128 sts]

Switch to larger needles and begin twisted stitch pattern.
Odd Rounds: [work Chart A, k1] repeat 6 (8) times
Even Rounds: knit
Work in this manner until you have completed rounds 1-28 of chart A, then proceed to decrease.

Decrease at crown following chart B, switching to double pointed needles when it becomes necessary.
Odd Rounds: [work chart B, k1] around
Even Rounds: knit
After round 11 of chart B, there will be 24 (32) sts.

Round 12: [sl1-k2tog-psso, k1] around   [12 (16) sts]
Round 13: ssk around   [6 (8) sts]

Break yarn, leaving a 6 inch tail. Thread tail through remaining live sts and pull tight to close top of hat. Weave in ends then block your hat to flatten the crown decreases. You can block the hat quite a bit larger and slouchier if desired.

key & abbreviations

☐ **k** - knit

☑ **k2tog** - knit two together

☒ **ssk** - slip, slip, knit

▨ **RT - right twist** - k2tog, leave sts on LH needle, then knit first st on LH needle, then slip both sts off LH needle at once.

▧ **LT - left twist** - skipping first st, knit second st on LH needle through back loop. Then knit both first and second sts on LH needle together through back loops, then slip both sts off LH needle at once.

M **m1** - make 1 stitch

chart B - decrease pattern

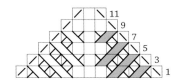

chart A - sitka pattern

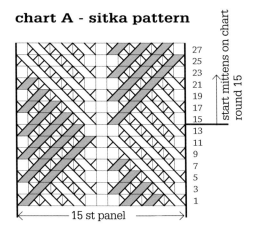

27
25
23
21
19
17
15
13
11
9
7
5
3
1

start mittens on chart round 15

← 15 st panel →

chart C - thumb gusset

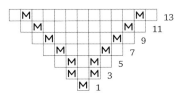

13
11
9
7
5
3
1

Large size: begin thumb gusset at round 17 of chart A
Medium size: begin thumb gusset at round 19 of chart A
Small size: begin thumb gusset at round 23 of chart A

Chart Notes:
Even numbered rounds are knit

sitka spruce mittens:

CO 32 (34,38) sts on smaller needles. PM and join for working in the round. Work 10 (10,16) rounds in twisted ribbing: (k1-tbl, p1) around. Switch to larger needles.

The mittens have the sitka pattern on the back of the hand, with a stockinette stitch palm and thumb.

For mittens, you begin the pattern on Round 15 of chart A, work to the end of the chart (Round 28), then work rounds 1-28 once more before proceeding to decrease pattern. Even numbered rounds: knit all sts.

Small & Medium Sizes: k1, work chart A, k1, place RH thumb marker, knit to end
Large Size: k2, work chart A, k2, place RH thumb marker, knit to end

To increase for thumb, begin Chart C as you work Chart A Round 17 (for Large), Round 19 (for Medium), or Round 23 (for Small). For LH mitten insert thumb gusset at the beginning of the round. For RH mitten, insert thumb gusset after RH thumb marker.

Work rounds 1-14 of Chart C, continuing with Chart A on back of hand as as established. After round 14 of chart C, you will place thumb sts on hold:

LH mitten: put first 13 sts on hold, work as established to end of round.
RH mitten: work as established to RH thumb marker, put next 13 sts on hold, work to end as established. Continue to work in the round to end of round 28 of chart A.

To decrease at fingertips:
k1(1,2), work chart B, k1(2,2), ssk, knit to last 2(3,4) sts, k2tog, k0(1,2). Even numberd rounds: knit. After round 11 of chart B, there will be 8 (10,14) sts.

Next Round: k1(1,2), sl1-k2tog-psso, k1(2,4), sl1-k2tog-psso, k0(1,2). Cut yarn, leaving a 6 inch tail. Thread tail through remaining sts and pull tight to close top of mitten.

Thumb: put held sts back on needles. Pick up 3 sts in body of mitten, then knit to 1 stitch before end. [16 sts] This is the new start of round.

Next Round: ssk, k1, k2tog, knit to end   [14 sts]

Knit every round until thumb is just short of desired length. To decrease: (k2tog) around   [7 sts]

Break yarn, draw end through remaining sts to close top of thumb. Weave in ends, block, and get out to explore the west coast wilderness!

irresistible earthy knits by Alexa Ludeman and Emily Wessel

lions gate

scrumptious and snuggly cabled cowl  *by Alexa Ludeman*

Vancouver is surrounded by water - bounded by a river, an inlet, and the Pacific. Bridges are one of the city's defining features. The most famous is the Lion's Gate: an elegant suspension bridge built in 1938 to link the urban centre with the north shore communities and wilderness beyond.

This architecturally-inspired cowl can be an exuberantly long piece to drape or wrap two or three times around your neck, or a short and luscious little neck warmer.

sizing: Large cowl wraps 2-3 times around, Small once
Finished cowl measures 9 (11) inches deep, 20 (58) inches around

materials:

Yarn: 200 (500) yds worsted / aran weight yarn
(we used Blue Sky Alpacas Worsted Hand Dyes in 'ecru' and 'olive')

Needles: US #9 / 5.5 mm *(or as required to meet gauge)*;
circular needles; 16" for small, 32"+ for large

Gauge: 16 sts / 4"   *(gauge in stockinette stitch)*

Notions: cable needle, stitch markers, darning needle

pattern:

The cowl is knit in the round. CO 96 (264) sts. Join for working in the round, being careful not to twist stitches.

Twisted Ribbing: (k1-tbl, p1) around
Work in twisted ribbing as established for 1.5 (2.5) inches.

Proceed to work cable pattern following chart A or text instructions. Work rounds 1-20, then rounds 1-17 once more. Work in twisted ribbing for 1.5 (2.5) inches. Bind off loosely, weave in ends and block lightly.

chart A - lions gate cable

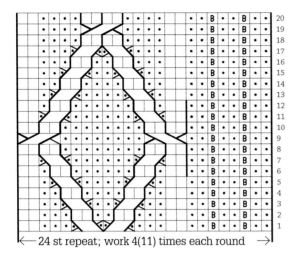

←— 24 st repeat; work 4(11) times each round —→

key & abbreviations

☐ **k** - knit

B **k1-tbl** - knit through back loop

· **p** - purl

 t3f (twist 3 front) - slip next 2 sts onto cn and hold in front of work, p1 from LH needle, k2 from cn

t3b (twist 3 back) - slip next st onto cn and hold in back of work, k2 from LH needle, p1 from cn

c4f (cable 4 front) - slip next 2 sts onto cn and hold in front of work. K2 from LH needle then k2 from cn

c4b (cable 4 back) - slip next 2 sts onto cn and hold in back of work. K2 from LH needle then k2 from cn

lions gate cable:

Round 1: [(p2, k1-tbl) twice, p2, k2, p3, t3b, t3f, p3, k2] around
Round 2: [(p2, k1-tbl) twice, p2, k2, p3, k2, p2, k2, p3, k2] around
Round 3: [(p2, k1-tbl) twice, p2, k2, p2, t3b, p2, t3f, p2, k2] around
Round 4: [(p2, k1-tbl) twice, p2, k2, p2, k2, p4, k2, p2, k2] around
Round 5: [(p2, k1-tbl) twice, p2, k2, p1, t3b, p4, t3f, p1, k2] around
Round 6: [(p2, k1-tbl) twice, p2, k2, p1, k2, p6, k2, p1, k2] around
Round 7: [(p2, k1-tbl) twice, p2, k2, t3b, p6, t3f, k2] around
Round 8: [(p2, k1-tbl) twice, p2, k4, p8, k4] around
Round 9: [(p2, k1-tbl) twice, p2, c4f, p8, c4b] around
Round 10: as round 8
Round 11: [(p2, k1-tbl) twice, p2, k2, t3f, p6, t3b, k2] around
Round 12: as round 6
Round 13: [(p2, k1-tbl) twice, p2, k2, p1, t3f, p4, t3b, p1, k2] around
Round 14: as round 4
Round 15: [(p2, k1-tbl) twice, p2, k2, p2, t3f, p2, t3b, p2, k2] around
Round 16: as round 2
Round 17: [(p2, k1-tbl) twice, p2, k2, p3, t3f, t3b, p3, k2] around
Round 18: [(p2, k1-tbl) twice, p2, k2, p4, k4, p4, k2] around
Round 19: [(p2, k1-tbl) twice, p2, k2, p4, c4b, p4, k2] around
Round 20: as round 18

torrent

watery lace socks *by Emily Wessel and Alexa Ludeman*

The Pacific Northwest is a rainy place. While people hurry gore-tex clad through city streets, in the mountains the snow accumulates, blanketing massive icefields that stretch north to Alaska.

These pretty lacy socks are inspired by glacier-fed torrents which flow from mountaintops to sheltered coves, carving out watery paths as they gurgle and rumble to the sea.

sizing: Adult S (M, L)
Finished circumference: 7.5 (8, 8.5) inches
Length is adjustable

materials:

Yarn: 370 (400, 420) yds sock weight yarn
(sample shown in Madelinetosh Tosh Sock in 'glacier')

Gauge: 32 sts / 4" in stockinette stitch

Needles: US #1 / 2.25mm; double pointed needles or a long circular needle, as desired for knitting in the round

Notions: stitch markers, darning needle

pattern:

These socks are knit in the round from cuff to toe, with standard heel flap, short row heel and gusset construction. They are knit in stockinette stitch with a lace panel which runs down the leg onto the foot. Length is adjustable.

cuff: CO 60 (64,68) sts loosely, PM and join for working in the round. Work in 2x2 ribbing: (k2, p2) around for 1 inch.

leg: Work setup round: k20 (22,24), PM, knit to end

Odd Rounds: knit to marker, work chart A, knit to end
Even Rounds: knit *(even rounds of chart A are knit)*

Work rounds 1-40 of chart A one time, then rounds 1-38 once more.

heel flap: k16, turn work so that WS is facing. Sl1, p31 all onto a single needle. Heel flap is worked back and forth on these 32 sts, with the remaining 28 (32,36) sts on hold for instep.

Row 1 (RS): Sl1, k31
Row 2 (WS): Sl1, p31

Repeat rows 1 and 2 a total of 16 times. There will be 16 slipped sts along each edge of the heel flap.

chart A - wave lace panel

39
37
35
33
31
29
27
25
23
21
19
17
15
13
11
9
7
5
3
1

← —————— 20 stitch panel —————— →

key & abbreviations

☐	**k** - knit
Ⓞ	**yo** - yarn over
Ⓜ	**m1** - make 1
╱	**k2tog** - knit 2 together
╲	**ssk** - slip, slip, knit
◣	**sssk** - slip, slip, slip, k3tog through back loops

Chart Notes:
Even numbered rounds are knit

heel turn:

Row 1(RS): sl1, k18, ssk, k1, turn work
Row 2: sl1, p7, p2tog, p1, turn work
Row 3: sl1, knit to 1 stitch before the gap, ssk
(this combines 1 st from each side of the gap), k1, turn work
Row 4: sl1, purl to 1 st before the gap, p2tog
(this combines 1 st from each side of the gap), p1, turn

Repeat rows 3-4 until all sts have been worked. [20 sts]
Knit 10 and PM to indicate new start of round. Proceed to Gusset.

gusset: instructions for 3 dpns: **N1**, **N2**, **N3**

Round 1: **N1** - k10, pick up 16 sts along side edge of heel flap,
N2 - work as established [k4(6,8),work chart A, k4(6,8)],
N3 - pick up 16 sts along edge of heel, k10 [80 (84,**88**) sts]
Round 2: knit all sts
Round 3: **N1** - knit to last 3 sts, k2tog, k1, **N2** - work in pattern as set
N3 - k1, ssk, knit to end [2 sts dec]
Round 4: knit all sts

Repeat rounds 3 and 4 until 60 (64,68) sts remain.

foot: Continue working stockinette and lace panel as set until foot is 1.5 inches short of desired length.

toe: Knit 15 (16,17) sts and stop. This is the new start of round. From this point redistribute sts as follows: 30 (32,34) sts on **N1**, 15 (16,17) sts on **N2**, 15 (16,17) sts on **N3**.

Round 1: knit
Round 2: **N1** - k1, ssk, knit to 3 sts before end of needle, k2tog, k1
N2 - k1, ssk, knit to end
N3 - knit to last 3 sts, k2tog, k1 [4 sts dec]

Repeat rounds 1-2 until there are 40 sts. Then repeat round 2 until there are 24 sts. Place first 12 sts on one needle, and remaining 12 sts on a second. Graft toe closed using kitchener stitch, weave in all ends, and block your socks to show the lace pattern to the best effect!

irresistible earthy knits by Alexa Ludeman and Emily Wessel

cable A: repeat rows 1-20

Rows 1, 3, 5, 7 (RS):	knit 8
Rows 2, 4, 6, 8 (WS):	purl 8
Row 9:	c4b, c4f
Rows 10, 12, 14, 16, 18:	(p1, k1) 3 times, k2
Rows 11, 13, 15, 17:	(k1, p1) 3 times, p2
Row 19:	as row 9
Row 20:	as row 2

cable B: repeat rows 1-20

Rows 1, 3, 5, 7 (RS):	(k1, p1) 3 times, k2
Rows 2, 4, 6, 8 (WS):	(p1, k1) 3 times, p2
Row 9:	c4b, c4f
Rows 10, 12, 14, 16, 18:	purl 8
Rows 11, 13, 15, 17:	knit 8
Row 19:	as row 9
Row 20:	as row 2

seeded cable charts

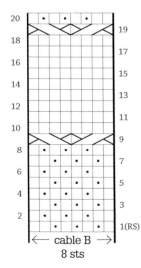

cable B
8 sts

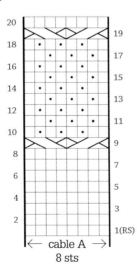

cable A
8 sts

key & abbreviations

☐   **k** - knit on RS / purl on WS

•   **p** - purl on RS / knit on WS

c4f (cable 4 front) - slip next 2 sts onto cn and hold in front of work. K2 from LH needle then k2 from cn

c4b (cable 4 back) - slip next 2 sts onto cn and hold in back of work. K2 from LH needle then k2 from cn

Chart Notes: RS (odd #) chart rows are read from R to L, and WS rows are read from L to R. The key indicates how symbols are to be read on RS and WS

sea to sky

cabled blanket in shifting colours  *by Alexa Ludeman*

A big part of what it means to live in Vancouver is being close to the ocean, the forest, and the mountains. There is nothing better than looking across the water to the majestic peaks of the North Shore. This blanket was inspired by the road to Whistler, along the Sea to Sky highway. The road curves along a sheer slope with peaks to one side and a drop to the Pacific on the other.

sizing: Baby Blanket (Afghan, Big Ass Blanket)
Finished size: 32 (42, 55) inches square
Width can be adjusted by adding or subtracting a multiple of 24 sts at cast on. Length can be adjusted knitting longer or shorter.

materials: Sample shown was knit from 2 strands of sock yarn held together. One is a variegated colourway which is used throughout the blanket. The other is a series of semi-solid colourways which shift from golden to blue.

Yarn: 1600 (3200, 4800) yds sock yarn **held doubled** or
800 (1600, 2400) yds worsted / aran weight yarn
(we used Indigo Moon Merino Superwash in various colours)

Needles: US #9 / 5.5 mm *(or as required to meet gauge)*

Gauge: 16 sts / 4" *(gauge in stockinette stitch)*

Notions: cable needle, darning needle

pattern:

CO 132 (180, 228) sts. Establish seed stitch: (k1, p1) repeat to end
Repeat this row for 2.5".

Blanket has 10-st seed-stitch borders either side, and cables which are separated by 4-st purl sections. The cable pattern is a 20-row repeat. Work pattern as follows, referring to charts or written instructions for cable A and cable B.

RS rows: (k1,p1) 5 times, p4, [work cable A, p4, work cable B, p4] repeat to last 18 sts, work cable A, p4, (k1,p1) 5 times

WS rows: (k1,p1) 5 times, k4, [work cable A, k4, work cable B, k4] repeat to last 18 sts, work cable A, k4, (k1,p1) 5 times

Continue as established in pattern until piece is 2.5 inches short of desired length, ending on cable rows 6 or 12. Work in seed stitch for 2.5 inches. Bind off loosely and block your blanket to show off the pretty cables!

tofino surfer

post waves warmer *by Alexa Ludeman*

Tofino, BC is the place to surf and be seen on the western shore of Vancouver Island. In summer the beach is packed with tourists and hippies. Everyone is trying to get on a surfboard and show their stuff: most of us inexperienced individuals looking more like floundering seals than sleek gods of the water! Of course, beach fashion cannot be ignored in this environment. It is crucial to look cool after hitting the waves, right? Surfing north of the 49th means wet suits in August so aprés surf a warm toque is needed by the beach bonfire!

The Tofino Surfer toque can be knit as a simple beanie or slouchy hat or you can add all the bells and whistles: earflaps, tassels, and pompoms - whatever your groove is.

sizing: Baby (Child, Adult S, M, L) beanie or slouch styles
Head Circumference: 16 (18, 20, 22, 24) inches

materials:

Yarn:	Bulky weight or DK weight held double
beanie :	100 (120, 160, 180, 200) yds
slouch:	120 (150, 180, 220, 240) yds
	To make earflaps, tassles and pompom requires 50 yds more
	(we used Berocco Vintage DK held double in '21106-Bubble' and '21107-Pool Party')
Needles:	US #10 / 6 mm *(or as required to meet gauge)*
	16" circular and double pointed needles
Gauge:	16 sts / 4" *(gauge in stockinette stitch)*
Notions:	cable needle, darning needle

pattern:

This hat is knit in the round from brim to crown. CO 64 (72,80,88,96) sts and join for working in the round.

Ribbing: (k2, p2) around
Work in ribbing until piece measures 1 (1.5, 2, 2, 2) inches from cast on.

Cable Setup: (k6, p2) around
Repeat this round 2 more times.

tofino cable pattern (10 round repeat)

Rounds 1, 3, and 5: (c3b, c3f, p2) around
Rounds 2, 4, and 6-10: (k6, p2) around

For Beanie: Repeat rounds 1-10 of Tofino cable pattern 2 (2, 3, 3, 3) more times, work rounds 1-6 once more then proceed to decreases.

For Slouch: Repeat rounds 1-10 of Tofino cable pattern 3 (3, 4, 4, 4) more times, work rounds 1-6 once more then proceed to decreases.

decreases

Round 1: (k6, p2tog) around
Round 2: (k6, p1) around
Round 3: (ssk, k2, k2tog, p1) around
Round 4: (k4, p1) around
Round 5: (ssk, k2tog, p1) around
Round 6: (k2tog, p1) around
Round 7: (k2tog) around

Break yarn, leaving a 6 inch tail. Thread tail through remaining live stitches and pull tight. Weave in ends.

earflaps: Pick up 12 (14,16,18,20) sts along the inside of the hat at the top of the ribbing. Knit 8 (10,12,12,14) rows.

Next Row: k1, ssk, knit to last 3 sts, k2tog, k1
Next Row: knit
Repeat these 2 rows until 6 sts remain.

Next Row: k2, yo, k2tog, k2
Next Row: knit
Bind off all stitches.

Work second earflap the same, opposite first.

braids & tassels: Cut several lengths of yarn 2.5 times the desired length of the braid. Thread these through the yarn over opening in the earflap, braid and knot.

pompom: Make pompom and attach securely to the top of hat.

chart A - tofino cable

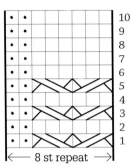

Chart Notes: Read charts from R to L. Refer to written instructions for number of chart repeats to work for each size.

key & abbreviations

☐ **k** - knit

• **p** - purl

c3b - **cable 3 back** - slip 2 sts to cn, hold in back of work. k1 from LH needle, k2 from cn

c3f - **cable 3 front** - slip 1 st to cn, hold in front of work. k2 from LH needle, k1 from cn

irresistible earthy knits by Alexa Ludeman and Emily Wessel

campfire

snuggly shawl collar for campfire nights *by Alexa Ludeman and Emily Wessel*

What's cuter than father-son matching sweaters? Eating smores while wearing them around the campfire on the family camping trip! Lets have some ghost stories!

sizing: The pattern includes 6 child and 9 adult sizes: 0-1 yrs (1-2 yrs, 3-4 yrs, 5-7 yrs, 8-10 yrs, 11-13 yrs, **mens XXS, XS, S, M, L, XL, XXL, 3XL, 4XL**). Child sizes are knit in DK weight yarn and adult sizes are knit in Worsted / Aran weight yarn.

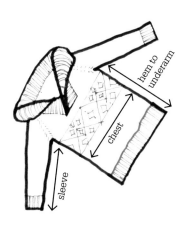

Size	Chest	Sleeve	Hem to UA	Yardage MC	CC1, 2
0-1 yrs	19.5"	8.5"	8"	350	50 ea
1-2 yrs	21.5"	9.5"	10"	400	60 ea
3-4 yrs	24"	11"	12"	500	70 ea
5-7 yrs	26"	12"	13"	650	80 ea
8-10 yrs	27.5"	14"	14"	800	100 ea
11-13 yrs	29.5"	16"	16"	900	120 ea
mens XXS	33"	18"	16"	900	120 ea
mens XS	35.5"	18.5"	17"	1000	140 ea
mens S	37.5"	18.5"	18"	1100	160 ea
mens M	40"	19"	19"	1200	180 ea
mens L	44.5"	20"	19"	1300	200 ea
mens XL	46.5"	20"	20"	1450	220 ea
mens XXL	48.5"	20"	22"	1600	240 ea
mens 3XL	55"	21"	23"	1700	250 ea
mens 4XL	60"	21"	23"	1900	260 ea

materials: Main Colour (MC) and 2 Contrast Colours (CC1,2)

	CHILDRENS sizes	ADULT sizes
Yarn	DK weight yarn (yardage listed above)	Worsted / Aran weight yarn (yardage listed above)
Gauge	22 sts / 4"	18 sts / 4"
Needles	US #4 / 3.5mm and US #6 / 4.0 mm *or as req'd to meet gauge*	US #6 / 4.0 mm and US #8 / 5.0 mm

Notions: stitch markers, darning needle

(samples shown in Sweet Georgia Superwash DK and Worsted, in 'espresso', 'bison', and 'tumbled stone')

pattern: This pullover is knit from the bottom up, in the round. Body and sleeves are knit to underarm, then joined for working the yoke. The shawl collar is picked up and knit last.

sleeves: (make 2 the same)

Using MC and smaller needles CO 32 (32,36,36, 40,40,**36,36,40,44,48,52,52,56,56**) sts and join for working in the round. Work in 2x2 ribbing for 1.5 (1.5, 1.5, 2, 2, 2, **2, 2, 2, 2, 2, 2, 2.5, 2.5, 2.5**) inches. 2x2 ribbing is (k2, p2) around. Switch to larger needles and knit 2 rounds.

Increase round: k2, m1, knit to last 2 sts, m1, k2 Knit 4 rounds.

Continue to knit in stockinette, working an increase round every 5th round, until there are 38 (40,46,48,50,56,**52,54,58,62,68,72,74,78,88**) sts. Work even until sleeve measures 8.5 (9.5, 11, 12, 14, 16, **18, 18.5, 18.5, 19, 20, 20, 20, 21, 21**) inches (or desired length).

To prepare for joining arms to body, place the first and last 3 (3,4,4,4,4,**4,4,4,4,5,5,5,6,6**) sts of the round on waste yarn (for underarm), and the remaining sts on a separate piece of waste yarn. Break yarn and set sleeve aside.

body: Using MC and smaller needles, CO 108 (120,132,144,148,160,**148,160,168,180,200,208, 220,248,268**) sts and join for working in the round. Work in 2x2 ribbing for 1.5 (1.5, 1.5, 1.5, 2, 2, **2, 2, 2.5, 2.5, 2.5, 2.5, 3, 3, 3**) inches.

Switch to larger needles and knit next round, increasing 0 (0,0,0,2,2,**2,0,2,0,0,2,0,2,2**) sts evenly spaced [108 (120,132,144,150,162,**150, 160,170,180,200,210,220,250,270**) sts]. Work in stockinette stitch until body measures 4.5 (6.5, 8.5, 9.5, 10.5, 12.5, **8.5, 9.5, 10.5, 11.5, 11.5, 12.5, 13.5, 14.5, 14.5**) inches. (or 3.5 / 7.5 inches short of desired length for child / adult sizes)

Begin fair-isle pattern. *It is important that you achieve the same gauge in your fair-isle section as you had in the stockinette stitch portion of the body. If you tend to knit at a tighter gauge when working fair-isle, try using a larger needle for the colourwork.*

Using CC1 and CC2, work rounds 1-23 of Charts A and B or rounds 1-39 of Charts C and D as indicated for your chosen size.

0-12 mo: [work chart A, work chart B] around

1-2 yrs: [work chart A] around

3-4 yrs: [work chart B once, work chart A twice] around

5-7 yrs: [work chart B twice, work chart A twice] around

8-10 yrs: [work chart A] around

11-13 yrs: work chart A three times, chart B once, chart A twice, chart B once

XXS: [work chart C] around

XS: work chart C three times, work chart D once

S: work chart C twice, chart D once, chart C once, chart D once

M: [work chart D, work chart C] around

L: [work chart C] around

XL: chart C three times, work chart D once, chart C once

XXL: [work chart D once, chart C twice] around

3XL: [work chart C] around

4XL: work chart C three times, chart D once, chart C once, chart D once

After completing the final chart row, switch to MC and knit 2 rounds.

Child Size Charts - work rows 1-23 one time

chart B   chart A

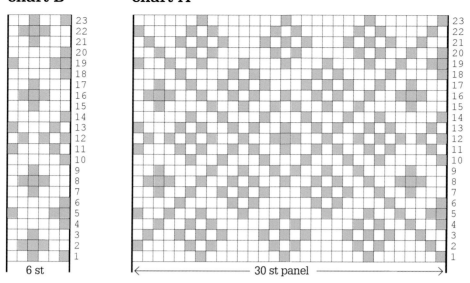

6 st   30 st panel

Adult Size Charts - work rows 1-39 one time

chart D   chart C

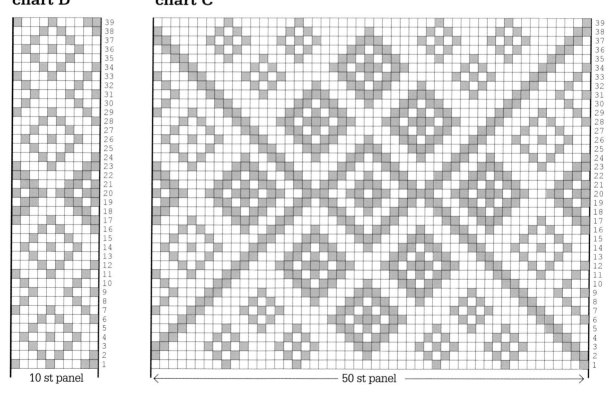

10 st panel   50 st panel

key & abbreviations

☐ **CC1** - contrast colour 1 (knit)

▨ **CC2** - contrast colour 2 (knit)

Chart Notes: Charts A and B are for Child Sizes, Charts C and D are for Adult Sizes.

yoke: To work the yoke you will join arms and body onto a single needle.

In preparation for working the yoke, you will move the beginning of round to centre front. To do this, knit 33 (30,36,48,60,45,**50,75,50,35,50, 50,60,100,75**) stitches, stop, PM. This is the new start of round, which is located at centre front.

Flatten out your body tube and take a look at the positioning of the pattern, and how it looks at centre front. If you would prefer to align the pattern in a different place, now is the point where you can make this change.

To join body and sleeves:

Knit 24 (27,29,32,34,37,**34,36,39,41,45,48,50,57,62**) body sts (the right half of the front), PM.

Put next 6 (6,8,8,8,8,**8,8,8,8,10,10,10,12,12**) body sts on hold (right underarm).

Knit 32 (34,38,40,42,48,**44,46,50,54,58,62,64,66,76**) arm sts from right sleeve, PM.

Knit 48 (54,58,64,67,73,**67,72,77,82,90,95,100, 113,123**) body sts (back), PM.

Put next 6 (6,8,8,8,8,**8,8,8,8,10,10,10,12,12**) body sts on hold (left underarm).

Knit stitches from left sleeve as from right, PM.

Knit remaining 24 (27,29,32,33,36,**33,36,38,41,45, 47,50,56,61**) body sts (the left half of the front).

There are now 160 (176,192,208,218,242,**222,236, 254,272,296,314,328,358,398**) sts on a single needle, and the start of round is at centre front.

yoke shaping: You will now begin to work paired decreases at the 4 marked points, to shape the yoke. This will decrease 8 sts every 2nd round (or row) throughout the yoke.

Round 1: knit
Round 2: (knit to 3 sts before marker, ssk, k2, k2tog) repeat 4 times, knit to end

Repeat rounds 1-2 a total of 2 (2,3,4,5,5,**3,3,3,3,4, 4,4,4,4**) times. [144 (160,168,176,178,202, **198,212,230,248,264,282,296,326,366**) sts]

Knit 1 more round, stopping 6 (8,8,8,9,9,**8,9,9,10, 10,10,11,11,11**) sts before the end of the round.

Now BO the first 12 (16,16,16,19,19,**17,18,19,20, 20,21,22,23,23**) sts. These BO sts are centred on the front of the pullover. Proceed to the end of the row, working paired decreases at the 4 marked raglan points as established, and knit to the BO sts, at which point you can knit no further! From now on you will work in rows. Turn work, and purl 1 row. [124 (136,144,152,151, 175,**173,186,203,220,236, 253,266,295,335**) sts]

From this point on continue working paired decreases at each marker, while at the same time decreasing sts to shape the neckline.

Row 1 (yoke plus neckline decrease): k1, ssk, (knit to 3 sts before marker, ssk, k2, k2tog) four times, knit to last 3 sts, k2tog, k1   [10 sts dec]
Row 2 (WS): purl
Row 3 (yoke decrease): (knit to 3 sts before first marker, ssk, k2, k2tog) four times, knit to end [8 sts dec]
Row 4: purl
Row 5: as row 3
Row 6: purl

Repeat Rows 1-6 a total of 2 (2,3,4,3,4,**4,5,5,6,6,6, 7,7,9**) times. [72 (84,66,48,73,71,**69,56,73,64,80, 97,84,113,101**) sts]. Then repeat rows 3-4 an additional 4 (5,2,0,3,2,**2,0,2,0,1,3,1,4,2**) times. [40 (44,50,48,49,55,**53,56,57,64,72,73,76,81,85**) sts] Remove markers, place remaining sts on hold and break yarn.

irresistible earthy knits by Alexa Ludeman and Emily Wessel

shawl collar: Collar is worked using smaller needles and MC. With RS facing, start at the juncture between the horizontal BO sts at centre front, and the R neckline edge. Pick up 21 (25,25,25,26,30,**30,31,36,37,39,44,45,52,60**) sts *(approx 1 in every row)*, along the R neckline edge. Place held body sts back on needle, PM, kf&b across held sts *(this doubles the sts in this section)*, PM. Pick up same number of sts along L neckline edge as at R.

Ribbing (WS): (p2, k2) to last 2 st, p2
Work 2 more rows as established in ribbing.

Work Short Rows:
Work in pattern to 7 (8,8,8,8,10,**10,10,12,12,14, 14,16,18,20**) sts past 2nd marker, w&t
Work in pattern to 7 (8,8,8,8,10,**10,10,12,12,14, 14,16,18,20**) sts past the 1st marker, w&t
Work in pattern to 3 sts from the gap, w&t
Repeat last instruction a total of 8 (10,12,12,14, 16,**16,18,18,20,20,20,22,22,24**) times.

Next 2 rows: Work to the end of the row in pattern, picking up wrapped sts as you go.

The collar must be wide enough to stretch across the opening at centre front. Work in rib for 14 (20,20,20,26,26,**24,24,26,26,26,28,30,32,32**) more rows *(or more if required / desired)*. Bind off all sts knitwise on the RS. To encourage the collar to curl and stand up, bind off as usual to the 1st marker, then work each stitch k2tog before binding off: k2tog (k2tog, pass first stitch over second and off needles) repeat to second marker, then bind off as usual to end of row.

finishing: Overlap and sew down the edge of shawl collar to bind-off opening at centre front. Graft underarm stitches using kitchener stitch, and sew up little holes either end. Weave in all ends, and wet block sweater to even out the fair-isle stitch pattern.

Then grab some marshmallows, graham crackers and chocolate and head out to the campfire - mmmm s'mores!

mukluks

quick and bulky cowichan-inspired booties  *by Emily Wessel*

Winters can be cold and damp in our corner of the world. These chunky booties are perfect for high-speed sliding on hardwood floors, and cuddling up in front of the fire on a dark and stormy evening.

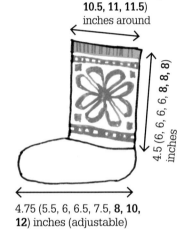

6 (6.5, 6.5, 7, 7.5, **10.5, 11, 11.5**) inches around

4.5 (6, 6, 6, 6, **8, 8, 8**) inches

4.75 (5.5, 6, 6.5, 7.5, **8, 10, 12**) inches (adjustable)

sizing: baby (toddler, child S, M, L, **adult S, M, L**)
   Ankle circumference: 6 (6.5, 6.5, 7, 7.5, **10.5, 11, 11.5**) inches
   While suggested lengths are included foot length is adjustable.
   Size can be adjusted by slightly fulling the finished bootie.

materials:

Yarn:

baby:	60 yds dk weight yarn in MC and CC
toddler, child:	90 yds aran weight yarn in MC and CC
adult S,M,L:	160 yds super bulky yarn in MC and CC

(samples in Debbie Bliss Donegal Luxury Tweed Aran, MC: 360010 CC: 360016 and Rowan Big Wool in 'white hot' and 'smokey')

Needles:

baby:	US #3 / 3.25 or 3.0 mm
toddler to child L:	US#5 / 3.75 mm
adult S,M,L:	US #10 / 6.0 mm

(or as required to meet gauge); double pointed needles

Gauge:

baby:	24 sts / 4" in stockinette stitch
toddler & child:	22 sts / 4" in stockinette stitch
adult S,M,L:	14 sts / 4" in stockinette stitch

Notions: stitch markers, darning needle

pattern: The foot is knit first, then sts are picked up from the ankle opening, and the leg is worked up to a ribbed cuff. A contrast colour sole can be knit flat and sewn on at the end.

foot: The bootie foot is knit from heel to toe. it is knit in rows until after the ankle opening then knit in rounds to the toe.

Using MC, CO 16 (16,18,20,22,**12,14,16**) sts.

Setup row (WS): p8(8,9,10,11,**7,7,8**), PM, purl to end
Next Row: knit to 1 st before marker, m1, k2, m1, knit to end
Next Row: purl
Repeat previous 2 rows two more times.
[22 (22,24,26,28,**18,20,22**) sts]

Knit 12 (12,14,16,16,**12,14,16**) rows in stockinette.

Next Row (RS): k1, m1, knit to last stitch, m1, k1
Next Row: purl
Repeat previous 2 rows two more times.
[28 (28,30,32,34,**24,26,28**) sts]

Next Row (RS): knit to end of row, then join to work in the round. Knit 21 (21,22,24,25,**18,20,21**), PM. This will be the new start of round. Knit in stockinette stitch rounds until foot is 4.25 (4.5, 5, 5.5, 6.5, 7, 9, 11) inches long, or 0.5 (1, 1, 1, 1, **1.25, 1.25, 1.5**) inches short of desired length.

toe: In preparation for toe, work setup round: k14 (14,15,16,17,**12,13,14**), PM, knit to end.

Next Round: k1, ssk, knit to 3 sts before marker, k2tog, k2, ssk, knit to last 3 sts, k2tog, k1
Next Round: knit
Repeat previous 2 rounds until 16 (16,18,16,18,**12,14,16**) sts remain.

Place first 8(8,9,8,9,**6,7,8**) sts on one needle, and remaining sts on another needle. Using kitchener stitch, graft sts from the 2 needles together to close toe. Fold the CO sts in half and sew together to close heel. Weave in ends before working the leg.

leg: next you will pick up sts around the ankle opening, and work the leg up from there.

Using MC start at heel with RS facing and pick up and knit 36(36,36,38,40,**36,38,40**) sts evenly spaced around ankle opening. Knit 2 rounds.

Using CC and MC, work rounds 1-3 of chart A. Knit 1 round in MC.
Using CC and MC, work rounds 1-17 of chart B. Knit 1 round in MC.
Using CC and MC, work rounds 1-3 of chart A. Knit 1 round in MC. Knit 1 round in MC, decreasing 0(0,0,2,0,**0,2,0**) sts, evenly spaced. [36(36,36,36,40,**36,36,40**) sts]
Switch to CC and knit 1 round. Knit 4 rounds in 2x2 ribbing [(k2,p2) around]. Bind off knitwise.

sole: the contrast colour sole is knit flat and sewn to the bottom of the bootie for cushion and durability. Make 2 the same.

Using CC, CO 8(8,9,10,11,**6,7,8**) sts. Purl 1 row.

Next Row: k1, m1, knit to last stitch, m1, k1
Next Row: purl
Repeat previous 2 rows until there are 16 (16,17,18,19,**14,15,16**) sts. Work even in stockinette stitch until sole is 0.5 (1, 1, 1, 1, **1.25, 1.25, 1.5**) inches short of desired length, ending with a WS row.

Next Row: k1, ssk, knit to last 3 sts, k2tog, k1
Next Row: purl
Repeat previous 2 rows until there are 8(8,9,10,11,**6,7,8**) sts. Bind off all sts on the RS. Sew the sole to the bottom of the bootie foot.

finishing: wet block the booties to even out the stitch pattern and allow the yarn to relax to its finished size. If the bootie seems too floppy or large, you can shrink it / stiffen it slightly by fulling it slightly. I recommend doing this in a bucket of hot soapy water, while wearing the booties (if you are an adult), or gently by hand for a child's booties. If you full the bootie in a washing machine be forewarned: the shrinkage can very quickly get out of hand!

chart A - band

3
2
1

2 st repeat

chart B - dogwood flower

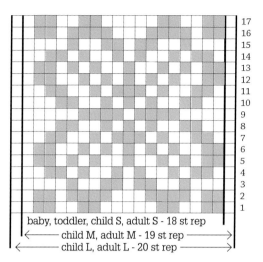

17
16
15
14
13
12
11
10
9
8
7
6
5
4
3
2
1

baby, toddler, child S, adult S - 18 st rep

← child M, adult M - 19 st rep →

← child L, adult L - 20 st rep →

key & abbreviations

☐ knit with MC (Main Colour)

▨ knit with CC (Contrast Colour)

Chart Notes: Charts are knit from R to L on each round and from round 1 to top. Work the portion of the chart indicated for your chosen size. Chart B is repeated twice each round.

university

perfectly preppy fingerless mitts  *by Alexa Ludeman*

Vancouver is a university town, full of students bounding about with their youthful optimism, questioning everything and re-inventing the world daily.

These preppy mittens are a great gift for the excited student heading off to university. They keep hands toasty when the air conditioning gets out of control in the library, or when you head out to the beach for a picnic and poetry reading.

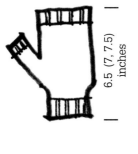

6 (7, 8) inches

6.5 (7, 7.5) inches

sizing: child (adult S, L)
Finished palm: 6 (7, 8) inches around
Finished length: 6.5 (7.0, 7.5) inches *(adjustable)*

materials:

Yarn: worsted / aran weight yarn
MC: 85 (90, 100) yds
CC: 50 (60, 70) yds
(sample shown in Rowan Lima in 'La Paz' and 'Andes')

Gauge: 24 sts / 4" in stockinette stitch using larger needles

Needles: US #4 / 3.75mm and US #6 / 4.0mm *(or as req'd to meet gauge);* double pointed needles

Notions: stitch markers, darning needle, waste yarn

pattern: These mitts are knit in the round from cuff to finger opening. Using MC and smaller needles CO 28 (32,40) sts, PM and join for working in the round.

2x2 Ribbing: (k2, p2) around
Work as established in 2x2 ribbing for 10 rounds. Change to larger needles.

Next Round: [k3(4,5), m1] 8 times, k4(0,0)
Next Round: m1, knit to end   [37 (41,49) sts]

Establish colourwork pattern with MC and CC: k1 in MC (this forms the vertical stripe at thumb), work chart A over the remaining 36 (40,48) sts.

Continue in pattern as set, working a total 3 repeats (12 rounds) of chart A.

Next begin to increase for thumb. The thumb gusset chart is worked at the start of the round, **taking the place of the first stitch of the round.** Over the next 9 rounds, work rounds 1-9 of chart B in place of the single MC knit stitch at the start of the round. Continue herringbone pattern as set over remainder of mitten.

Next round: place first 13 sts (thumb) on hold. CO 1 st in MC (this will be the first stitch of the round), join and work in pattern to end of round. [37 (41,49) sts]

Continue until a total of 7 (8, 9) repeats [28 (32,36) rows] of chart A have been worked *(or to desired length)*. Break CC, leaving a 6" tail. Change to smaller needles and continue in MC.

Decrease: [k2tog, k2(2,3)] 9 times, knit to end [28 (32,40) sts]

Work in 2x2 ribbing for 4 (4, 6) rounds. Bind off loosely and proceed to thumb.

thumb: Using larger needles place 13 thumb sts onto 3 needles. Knit across these 13 sts in established pattern then pick up 3 sts from mitten (1CC, 1MC, 1CC) [16 sts].

Join for working in the round. Work 4 rounds in pattern as established (1MC, 1CC stripes). Change to smaller needles and knit 1 round in MC. Work in 2x2 ribbing for 3 rounds. Bind off loosely, weave in ends. Make a second the same as the first, then and block mitts to even out the houndstooth pattern.

chart A -
houndstooth pattern

4 st rep

chart B -
thumb gusset

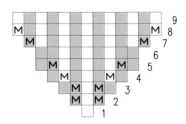

Chart Notes:
Charts are read from R to L, and from bottom to top. The houndstooth pattern repeats throughout body of mitten.

key & abbreviations

☐ **MC** - Main Colour (knit)

▨ **CC** - Contrast Colour (knit)

Ⓜ **m1** - make 1 stitch *(work in either MC or CC as indicated)*

irresistible earthy knits by Alexa Ludeman and Emily Wessel

urban hiker

zipped jacket with modern geometry  *by Emily Wessel*

This jacket is perfect for a stroll through Gas Town or Whistler Village, or perhaps a winter walk on the Sea Wall. Modern geometry, zipped front and a slim silouette make this the perfect man sweater. In a bulky yarn it knits up quickly so make maching cardigans for your adorable little man and your sexy old man too!

sizing: The pattern includes 6 child and 9 adult sizes:
1-2 yrs (2-3 yrs, 3-4 yrs, 5-7 yrs, 8-10 yrs, 11-13 yrs, **Mens XXS, XS, S, M, L, XL, XXL, 3XL, 4XL**)

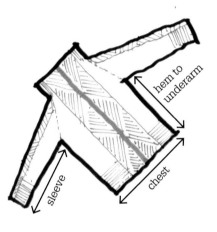

Size	Chest	Sleeve	Hem to UA	Yardage
1-2 yrs	22"	8.5"	7"	300
2-3 yrs	24"	9"	8"	380
3-4 yrs	25"	11"	10"	450
5-7 yrs	27"	14"	12"	600
8-10 yrs	29"	16"	14"	700
11-13 yrs	31"	17"	15"	800
XXS	33"	18"	16"	850
XS	35"	19"	16"	900
S	37"	19"	17"	1000
M	39"	20"	18"	1100
L	42"	20"	19"	1200
XL	46"	20"	19"	1300
XXL	51"	21"	20"	1450
3XL	56"	21"	20"	1600
4XL	60"	21"	20"	1700

materials:

Yarn: Bulky weight yarn - **refer to table for yardage**
(samples shown in Cascade Eco Wool '8018-silver')

Gauge: 16 sts / 4" in stockinette stitch

Needles: US #9 / 5.5mm; *(or as required to meet gauge)*
24" to 40" circular and double pointed needles

Notions: stitch markers, darning needle, zipper

pattern: This cardigan is knit seamlessly from the bottom up. After the body and arms are complete to underarm, they are joined onto one needle for the yoke, which is knit in rows through the collar. Lastly a zipper facing is worked on each front.

sleeves: The sleeves are knit in the round from cuff to underarm. A twisted stitch pattern is knit at the top of arm (work panel A for children's sizes, and panel B for adults sizes).

CO 26 (26,28,28,30,32,**38,42,44,44,46,48,50,50,50**) sts, PM and join for working in the round.

Setup round: p16(16,18,18,20,22,**26,30,32,32,34, 36,38,38,38**), k1, PM, knit to end

Round 1: knit to marker, work panel A1 or B1, k1
Round 2: purl to 1 st before marker, k1,
work panel as set, k1

Repeat rounds 1-2 a total of 6 (6,6,8,8,8,**12,12,12, 14,14,14,14,14,14**) times.

Move the start of round marker to the underarm: Remove start of round marker, knit 8 (8,9,9,10,11, **13,15,16,16,17,18,19,19,19**) sts, stop, and replace marker. This is the new start of round.

Work 2 rounds in pattern (knit to marker, work panel, knit to end). From here the sleeve is worked in stockinette stitch with panel at top of arm.

Increase round: k1, m1, work as established to last st, m1, k1   [2 sts inc]
Work 5 rounds even, then one increase round. Continue in this manner, working an increase round every 6th round, until there are 30 (34,36, 36,38,42,**46,48,50,56,58,62,68,74,76**) sts.

Work even until sleeve measures 8.5 (9, 11, 14, 16, 17, **18, 19, 19, 20, 20, 20, 21, 21, 21**) inches *(or desired length)*, ending with an even chart round.

Put the first and last 2 (3,3,3,3,4,**4,4,4,5,5,5,5,6,6**) sts of the round on hold (for underarm) and the remaining sts on hold separately. Break yarn.

Work the second sleeve the same as first, except work panels A2 or B2 at top of arm.

body: The body is worked in rows from hem to underarm. Mirrored twisted stitch patterns are worked at fronts (work panel B for child sizes, and panel C for adult sizes).

CO 78 (84,88,94,100,108,**116,122,128,134,144, 158,174,190,202**) sts.

Setup row (WS): p13(13,13,13,13,13,**17,17,17, 17,17,17,17,17,17**) sts, PM, knit to last 13 (13,13,13,13,13,**17,17,17,17,17,17,17,17,17**) sts, PM, knit to end

Row 1 (RS): k2, work panel B1 or C1, k1, knit to marker, k1, work panel B2 or C2, k2
Row 2:   purl to first marker, knit to second marker, purl to end *(WS of panels are purled)*
Repeat rows 1-2 a total of 8 (8,8,10,10,10,**14,14, 14,14,16,16,16,16,16**) times.

Next row (RS): Work in pattern to first marker, (k4, m1) a total of 12 (14,14,16,18,18,**18,20,22, 24,26,28,32,36,40**) times, knit remaining sts to second marker, work in pattern to end.
[90 (98,102,110,118,126,**134,142,150,158,170, 186,206,226,242**) sts]

Next Row (and all following WS rows): purl
Next Row (RS): work in pattern, continuing panels as set, and knitting all other sts

Continue working panels as set and stockinette stitch between them body measures 7 (8, 10, 12, 14, 15, **16, 16, 17, 18, 19, 19, 20, 20, 20**) inches *(or desired length)*, ending with a WS row.

join sleeves and body for yoke:

This row joins the body and sleeves onto a single needle. As you work the yoke, continue panels as set at fronts and sleeves.

Work 21 (22,23,25,27,28,**30,32,34,35,38,42,47,51, 55**) sts from body, place next 4 (6,6,6,6,8,**8,8,8,10, 10,10,10,12,12**) sts on hold (for underarm)

Work 26 (28,30,30,32,34,**38,40,42,46,48,52,58, 62,64**) sts from first sleeve (all except underarm sts), marking the **second** and **next-to-last** of these sts with a split-ring marker or safety pin, as this stitch will be the centreline of the raglan decrease shaping.

Work 40 (42,44,48,52,54,**58,62,66,68,74,82,92, 100,108**) sts from body, place next 4 (6,6,6,6,8,**8, 8,8,10,10,10,10,12,12**) sts on hold (for underarm)

Work sts from second sleeve as at first, marking the first and last of the sts in the same way.

Work remaining body sts to end of row.
[134 (142,150,158,170,178,**194,206,218,230,246, 270,302,326,346**) sts. Purl 1 row.

panel B2
40 row repeat

panel B1
40 row repeat

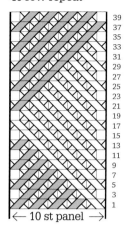

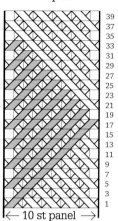

panel A2
32 row repeat

panel A1
32 row repeat

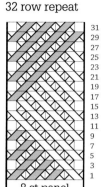

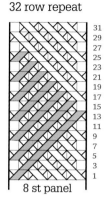

8 st panel

8 st panel

← 10 st panel →

← 10 st panel →

panel C2
56 row repeat

panel C1
56 row repeat

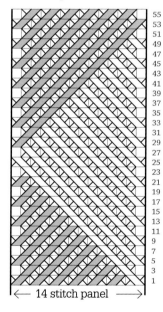

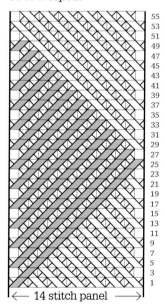

← 14 stitch panel →

← 14 stitch panel →

key & abbreviations

☐ **k** - knit

▨ **RT - right twist** - k2tog, leave sts on LH needle, then knit first st on LH needle, then slip both sts off LH needle at once.

⧄ **LT - left twist** - skipping first st, knit second st on LH needle through back loop. Then knit both first and second sts on LH needle together through back loops, then slip both sts off LH needle at once.

Chart Notes:
Charts are read from R to L.
On body and yoke, charts are knit in rows. On sleeves, charts are knit in the round. Only RS rows / odd numbered rounds are shown on charts. When knitting in rows, all WS rows: purl. When knitting in the round, all even numbered rounds: knit

yoke shaping: The yoke is shaped by raglan decreases at four points. At the stitches marked when the yoke was joined *(the second and next-to-last sts of the sleeve sections)*, work a double decrease to combine the marked stitch with the 2 stitches either side of it. This occurs every RS row. Continue panels as set.

Row 1 (RS): [work to 1 st before marked st, k3tog (the marked st, and one st from either side of it)] 4 times, decreasing at each of the 4 marked sts, then work as established to end.

Row 2 (WS): purl

Repeat rows 1-2 until 62 (62,62,70,74,82,**90,94,98,102,1 02,110,110,110,114**) sts remain, ending with a WS row.

As the arm and fronts decrease, in some sizes there will come a point where the decreases begin to encroach upon the stitch panel at the upper arm. When this occurs, simply work as much of the width of the panel as is possible (for example working the central 6 sts of the panel when only 6 sts remain) If you find this too confusing, simply switch to working stockinette once the panel no longer fits.

collar: A stand-up collar is worked on remaining sts.

Establish Ribbing: k2, continue panel, k1, work (p1, k1-tbl) to last 2 sts before marker, p2tog, k1, continue panel, k2.

Continue in pattern, working k1-tbl on both RS and WS of ribbing for a tight twisted rib.

Work in ribbing for a total of 10 (12,12,12,14,14,**16,16, 16,16,16,16,18,18,18**) rows *(or desired height)*. Bind off all but last stitch knitwise on a RS row.

facing: Leaving final collar stitch on needle, begin to pick up sts down LH front edge, with RS facing. Pick up 2 sts in every 3 rows. Knit 2 rows, purl 1 row, knit 1 row, purl 1 row, knit 1 row. Fold facing to inside, and sew live sts to back of work. Work RH facing the same. If you prefer buttons, you may opt to work a button band (perhaps in garter stitch or twisted rib) in place of the facing.

finishing: Using kitchener stitch, graft underarm sts, and sew up gaps at either end. Weave in all ends and block sweater. Wash zipper as you would wash the finished garment. Baste zipper into place, try cardigan on to check zipper location, then hand sew the zipper to facing.

irresistible earthy knits by Alexa Ludeman and Emily Wessel

chart A - main street cable

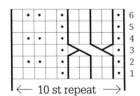

← 10 st repeat →

Chart Notes: read chart from R to L,
and from bottom to top.

key & abbreviations

☐ **k** - knit

• **p** - purl

⬗ **c4f** (cable 4 front) - slip
next 2 sts onto cn and hold
in front of work. K2 from
LH needle then k2 from cn

main street

knitwear for your beloved caffeinated bevy  *by Alexa Ludeman*

it's never too early to start an addiction...

There are many cities in the world with coffee culture, but in the Pacific Northwest perpetually overcast skies and rainy days make our daily caffeine intake a ritualized necessity.

When I meet up with friends we inevitably end up at one of about a million coffee shops, laughing and sipping (and often knitting). This coffee cozy fits with the bohemian vibe of Main Street. It is a great project for using up odds and ends, and makes a cute gift for your coffee companions!

sizing: One size fits most; 7" around by 4.5" tall

materials:

Yarn: 50 yds DK weight yarn
(we used Rowan Tweed in 'reeth' and 'wensley')

Needles: US #5 / 3.75 mm *(or as required to meet gauge)*

Gauge: 22 sts / 4"   *(gauge in stockinette stitch)*

Notions: cable needle, stitch markers, darning needle

pattern:

This cozy is knit from bottom to top with increases to fit the taper of a coffee cup. CO 32 sts, PM, and join for working in the round.

Work in 2x2 ribbing: (k2, p2) around for 6 rounds.

Next Round: (k4, m1) around   [40 sts]

Work 4 repeats of cable pattern, following Chart A or written instructions. *(This is a total of 24 rounds)*

Next round: (k10, m1) around   [44 sts]

Work in 2x2 ribbing for 6 rounds, then bind off loosely. Wrap it up with some gourmet beans as a cute gift for your favourite coffee drinker!

main street cable

Row 1:	[p1, k4] around
Row 2:	[p1, k4, p1, k1, p2, k1] around
Row 3:	[p1, c4f, p1, k4] around
Row 4:	as round 2
Row 5:	as round 1
Row 6:	as round 2

Vancouver is full of hipsters: tall guys in skinny jeans with no asses and chicks with artfully dishevelled hair and oversized glasses clad in ill-fitting coats and mismatched prints.

The hipster is clearly too cool for school, and they come by this nonchalant but epic style naturally, right? WRONG. They work at it EVERY DAY. It is NOT EASY.

This hat is the perfect knit for your favourite hipster: classic but a tiny bit edgy and inside-out looking, to maintain that 'I don't give a damn' ethos. Hipster can be knit in aran or DK weight yarn in sizes from proto-hipster baby to 'I wish I was still a hipster' Dad.

sizing: Baby (Child, **Adult S, M, L**)
Head circumference: 16 (18, **20, 21, 22**) inches

materials:

Yarn: Aran weight version: 60 (80,**90,110,120**) yds
DK weight version: 90 (110,**120,130,140**) yds
(we used Rowan Tweed in '589-hubberholme' and '590-wensley' and Debbie Bliss Donegal Luxury Tweed Aran in 'colour 15')

Needles: Aran version: US #6 / 4.0 mm and US #8 / 5.0 mm
DK version: US #4 / 3.5 mm and US #6 / 4.0 mm
(or as required to meet gauge);
16" circular and/or double pointed needles

Gauge: Aran version: 18 sts / 4"
DK version: 22 sts / 4"
(gauge in stockinette stitch using larger needles)

Notions: stitch markers, darning needle

hipster

a hat that's too cool for school  *by Alexa Ludeman*

pattern: This hat is knit in the round from brim to crown. It is knit inside out. Follow the instructions based on your chosen size and gauge option.

Using smaller needles, cast on.
Aran Version: CO 64 (72,**80,84,88**) sts
DK Version: CO 80 (88,**96,100,104**) sts

Join for working in the round and PM to indicate start of round.

Establish Ribbing: (k2, p2) around
Work as established in ribbing for 1 (1, **1.5, 1.5, 1.5**) inches.

Change to larger needles and knit 1 round. Continue in stockinette stitch (knitting every round) until piece measures 5 (6, **6.5, 7, 7.5**) inches.

crown decreases: Switch to double pointed needles for decreasing the top of the hat.

Aran Version: place 16 (18,**20,21,22**) sts on each of 4 needles
DK Version: place 20 (22,**24,25,26**) sts on each of 4 needles

Round 1: (p1, p2tog, knit to last 3 sts of needle, ssp, p1) repeat for remaining 3 needles
Round 2: (p2, knit to last 3 sts of needle, p2) repeat for remaining 3 needles

Repeat rounds 1 and 2 until there are:
Aran version: 8 (8,**8,9,8**) sts on each needle
DK version: 12 (12,**12,13,12**) sts on each needle

Then repeat round 1 until there are 4 (4,**4,5,4**) sts on each needle.

Adult M size ONLY: (p1, p3tog, p1) repeat for remaining 3 needles

Break yarn leaving a 6 inch tail. Thread tail through remaining live stitches and pull tight. Weave in ends and block hat. Wear with an attitude of cool apathy to perfect your hipster style.

false creek

deliciously chunky lace button scarf   by Emily Wessel

False Creek is an inlet at the heart of Vancouver. It is ringed by the Seawall: a path and park system which celebrates the city's proximity to the water. Ice cream, dog walking, sun bathing, and a farmers market only a short walk from your apartment: this is part of why Vancouver is consistently voted one of the most liveable cities in the world.

If you are a new knitter, or in need of a quick project this zippy little button scarf is an opportunity to learn about reading charts and working very basic lace stitches. In a super-bulky yarn False Creek works up quickly, making a perfect gift.

sizing: 9 inches tall by 26 inches long - One size fits all; but if you knit this bulky bad-boy in a slightly thicker or thinner yarn, or with slightly bigger or smaller needles, the finished size will vary.

materials: we suggest a super-bulky, but the scarf may also be knit using worsted or aran weight held double or triple.

Yarn:	90 yds super bulky weight yarn (8-10 sts/4") *(we used Malabrigo Rasta in '63-natural')*
Needles:	US #15 / 10 mm *(or as required to meet gauge)*
Gauge:	9 sts / 4" *(in stockinette stitch)*
Notions:	stitch markers, darning needle, 3 buttons

pattern: The cowl is knit from end to end. A garter stitch border surrounds the textured lace pattern.

CO 18 sts. Knit 7 rows.

Work the False Creek lace pattern following chart A or written instructions. The pattern consists of a 3-st garter edge, textured lace pattern over the centre 12 sts, then another 3-st garter edge.

To work from chart:

RS and WS rows: k3, work chart A, k3

Work rows 1-20 following chart A or written instructions a total of three times, then work rows 1-10 one more time. (70 rows)

Knit 2 rows.

Work buttonhole row: (k3, yo, k2tog) to last 3 sts, k3

Knit 4 more rows. Bind off, block scarf, and sew on funky buttons to correspond with buttonholes.

chart A - false creek lace

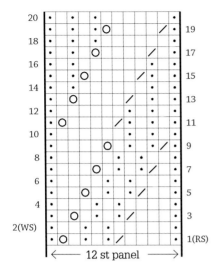

← 12 st panel →

key & abbreviations

☐ **k** - knit on RS, purl on WS

• **p** - purl or RS, knit on WS

Ⓞ **yo** - yarn over

╱ **k2tog** - knit 2 together

Chart Notes:

Chart illustrates only the lace pattern (the 3-st garter border either side of the lace pattern is not shown)

Chart shows both RS and WS rows. Read RS rows from right to left, and WS rows from left to right. Refer to key: as you will see, symbols indicate different stitches depending on whether they are worked on a RS or a WS row.

False Creek Button Scarf:

Note: written instructions describe the 3-st garter border as well as the textured lace panel shown in chart A.

Row 1(RS): k3, p1, k4, k2tog, p1, k1, p1, k1, yo, p1, k3
Row 2: k4, p2, k1, p1, k1, p5, k4
Row 3: k3, p1, k3, k2tog, p1, k1, p1, k1, yo, k1, p1, k3
Row 4: k4, p3, k1, p1, k1, p4, k4
Row 5: k3, p1, k2, k2tog, p1, k1, p1, k1, yo, k2, p1, k3
Row 6: k4, p4, k1, p1, k1, p3, k4
Row 7: k3, p1, k1, k2tog, p1, k1, p1, k1, yo, k3, p1, k3
Row 8: k4, p5, k1, p1, k1, p2, k4
Row 9: k3, p1, k2tog, p1, k1, p1, k1, yo, k4, p1, k3
Row 10: k4, p6, k1, p1, k1, p1, k4
Row 11: k3, p1, k1, p1, k1, p1, k2tog, k4, yo, p1, k3
Row 12: k4, p6, k1, p1, k1, p1, k4
Row 13: k3, p1, k1, p1, k1, k2tog, k4, yo, k1, p1, k3
Row 14: k4, p1, k1, p6, k1, p1, k4
Row 15: k3, p1, k1, p1, k2tog, k4, yo, p1, k1, p1, k3
Row 16: k4, p1, k1, p6, k1, p1, k4
Row 17: k3, p1, k1, k2tog, k4, yo, k1, p1, k1, p1, k3
Row 18: k4, p1, k1, p1, k1, p6, k4
Row 19: k3, p1, k2tog, k4, yo, p1, k1, p1, k1, p1, k3
Row 20: k4, p1, k1, p1, k1, p6, k4

irresistible earthy knits by Alexa Ludeman and Emily Wessel

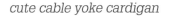

antler

cute cable yoke cardigan  *by Alexa Ludeman*

Nothing conjures up the Canadian Rockies like the image of antlers. The magestic rack of an Elk buck is something not many get to see in their lives and it is a sight to behold!

sizing: The pattern includes 7 child and 8 adult sizes:
0-6 mo (6-12 mo, 1-2 yrs, 2-4 yrs, 4-6 yrs, 6-8 yrs, 8-10 yrs, **adult XS, S, M, L, XL, XXL, 3XL, 4XL**)

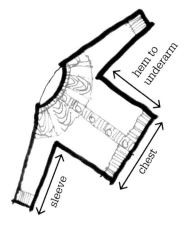

Size	Chest	Sleeve	Hem to UA	Yardage
0-6 mo	18"	7.5"	6"	280
6-12 mo	19"	8"	6.5"	330
1-2 yrs	20"	8.5"	7"	360
2-4 yrs	22"	10.5"	8"	440
4-6 yrs	24"	12"	10"	600
6-8 yrs	26"	14"	13"	700
8-10 yrs	28"	16"	15"	850
XS	31"	18"	15"	950
S	35"	19"	16"	1200
M	39"	19"	17"	1325
L	43"	20"	18"	1400
XL	47"	20"	18.5"	1500
XXL	51"	21"	19"	1600
3XL	55"	21"	20"	1700
4XL	59"	21"	20"	1800

materials:

Yarn: Worsted / Aran weight yarn - **refer to table for yardage** *(samples shown in Madelinetosh Tosh Vintage 'antler')*

Gauge: 18 sts / 4" in stockinette stitch using larger needles

Needles: US #6 / 4.0mm and US #8 / 5.0mm needles; *(or as required to meet gauge)* 24" circular and double pointed needles in both sizes

Notions: five to seven 3/4" buttons, cable needle, stitch markers, darning needle, waste yarn

pattern:
This cardigan is knit seamlessly from the bottom up. The body is worked in rows and the arms in the round. Button bands are worked last.

sleeves: work 2 the same

Using smaller needles CO 28(32,32,34,36,36,38,**40,40,42,46,48,50,54,54**) sts and join for working in the round. Work in 1x1 rib [(k1,p1) around] until piece measures 1 (1, 1, 1.5, 1.5, 1.5, 1.5, **1.5, 1.5, 2, 2, 2, 2, 2, 2**) inches. Switch to larger needles and knit 1 round.

Increase Round: k1, m1, knit to last st, m1, k1 Knit 5 rounds.

Repeat these 6 rounds until there are 30 (32,34, 36,40,44,46,**52,58,60,64,70,76,82,86**) sts.

Work even until sleeve measures 7.5 (8, 8.5, 10.5, 12, 14, 16, **18, 19, 19, 20, 20, 21, 21, 21**) inches *(or desired length)*.

To prepare for joining arms to body, place the first and last 3 (3,3,3,4,4,4,**4,4,4,5,5,5,6,6**) sts of the round on hold (for underarm), and the remaining sts on hold separately (for shoulders).

body:

Using smaller needles CO 79 (81,87,93,103,111, 121,**131,149,167,183,201,219,237,255**) sts.

Ribbing (RS): k2, (p1, k1) to last st, k1

Continue in ribbing until piece measures 1 (1, 1, 1.5, 1.5, 1.5, 1.5, **1.5, 1.5, 2, 2, 2, 2, 2, 2**) inches. Switch to larger needles and work in stockinette stitch until piece measures 6 (6.5, 7, 8, 10, 13, 15, **15, 16, 17, 18, 18.5, 19, 20, 20**) inches *(or desired length)* ending with a WS row.

join sleeves and body for yoke:
To join body and sleeves together onto a single needle:

Knit 15 (16,18,19,20,22,24,**27,31,36,38,43,47,51,55**) body sts. Put the next 6 (6,6,6,8,8,8,**8,8,8,10,10, 10,12,12**) body sts on hold (for underarm).

Knit 24 (26,28,30,32,36,38,**44,50,52,54,60,66,70,74**) held sts from one sleeve (all except underarm sts).

Knit next 37 (37,39,43,47,51,57,**61,71,79,87,95,105, 111,121**) sts from body. Put the next 6 (6,6,6,8,8,8, **8,8,8,10,10,10,12,12**) body sts on hold (underarm).

Knit held sts from second sleeve (except underarm sts). Knit remaining body sts. [115 (121,131,141,151,167,181,**203,233,255,271, 301,331,353,379**) sts]. Work 3 (3,3,3,3,3,3,**5,5,5,5, 5,5,5,5**) rows in stockinette stitch.

yoke: decrease to setup for cables

Next Row (RS): knit, decreasing 1(7,17,6,16,11,4, **5,14,15,10,19,28,29,34**) sts evenly spaced. [114 (114,114,135,135,156,177,**198,219,240,261,2 82,303,324,345**) sts] Purl 1 row.

Cable Setup Row (RS): k2, (p5, k16) repeat to last 7 sts, p5, k2

Next Row (WS): work in pattern as established; (knit the knits and purl the purls)

cable pattern:
the 16-st wide antler cable is worked between columns of purl sts as established in the **Cable Setup Row**. Continue to work these as purl sts as set. Six rows is one repeat of the antler cable pattern. Refer to chart and written instructions for antler cable.

RS rows: k2, [p5, work antler cable] repeat to last 7 sts, p5, k2

WS rows: work in pattern as established; (knit the knits and purl the purls)

Repeat the antler cable pattern (rows 1-6) as many times as indicated for your size:

0-6 mo to 1-2 yrs: work antler cable once (6 rows)

2-4 to 8-10 yrs: work antler cable twice (12 rows)

XS, S, M: work antler cable 3 times (18 rows)

L to 4XL: work antler cable 4 times (24 rows)

chart A - antler cable
repeat rows 1 - 6

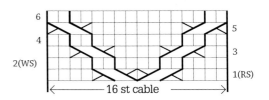

16 st cable

antler cable: repeat rows 1-6

Row 1 (RS):	k4, c4b, c4f, k4
Rows 2,4,6 (WS):	purl 16
Row 3:	k2, c4b, k4, c4f, k2
Row 5:	c4b, k8, c4f

key & abbreviations

☐ **k** - knit on RS / purl on WS

⊡ **p** - purl on RS / knit on WS

◿ **k2tog** - knit two together

◺ **ssk** - slip, slip, knit

◿ **p2tog** - purl 2 together

⊠ **c4b** - cable 4 back - slip 2 sts to cn, hold in back of work, k2 from LH needle, k2 from cn

⊠ **c4f** - cable 4 front - slip 2 sts to cn, hold in front of work, k2 from LH needle, k2 from cn

⊠ **c4bd** - cable 4 back decrease - slip 2 sts to cn, hold in back of work, k2 from LH needle, k2tog from cn

⊠ **c4fd** - cable 4 front decrease - slip 2 sts to cn, hold in front of work, ssk from LH needle, k2 from cn

▨ **NO STITCH**

yoke decreases: The top of the yoke is shaped by several decrease rows. Decreases occur in purl sections and within cables. Follow chart B and written instructions. All WS (even numbered) rows work as established. The 2 edge sts either side are worked in stockinette throughout.

Row 1 (first decrease): k2, [p1, p2tog twice, work antler cable] repeat to last 7 sts, p2tog twice, p1, k2

Row 3: work as established (row 3 of cable)

Row 5 (second decrease): work purl sts as set; at cables: c4bd, k2tog, k4, ssk, c4fd

Row 7: work purl sts as established; at cables: k2, c4b, c4f, k2

Row 9 (third decrease): k2, [p1, p2tog, c4b, k4, c4f,] repeat to last 4 sts, p2tog, p1, k2

Child sizes: stop working chart B after row 9. [76 (76,76,90,90,104,118) sts]. Next Row: purl, decreasing 16 (14,12,24,18,20,30) sts, evenly spaced *(work p2tog)*. [60 (62,64,66,72,84,88) sts]

Switch to smaller needles and work in 1x1 rib for 1 (1, 1, 1.5, 1.5, 1.5, 1.5) inches. Bind off knitwise on RS.

Adult sizes: Continue chart - Row 11: as row 7

Row 13 (fourth decrease): work purl sts as set; at cables: c4bd, k2tog, ssk, c4fd

After row 13 there are **96,106,116,126,136,146, 156,166**] sts. Purl 1 row, decreasing **0 (10,14,20, 26,28,38,48)** sts, evenly spaced *(work p2tog)*. [**96 (96,102,106,110,118,118,118)** sts]

Switch to smaller needles and work in 1x1 rib for **1.5 (1.5, 2, 2, 2, 2, 2, 2)** inches. Bind off knitwise on RS.

chart B - cable decreases -
work number of rounds indicated for your size

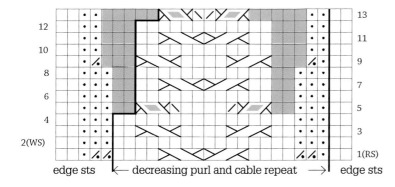

edge sts ← decreasing purl and cable repeat → edge sts

Chart Notes:
Child sizes: work chart rows 1-11.
Adult sizes, work chart rows 1-13
All WS rows: knit the knits and purl the purls.

button band: button bands are picked up either side of the front opening of the cardigan. Buttonholes may be worked on either side.

Using smaller needles, with RS facing, pick up approximately 4 sts in every 5 rows along front, ending with an odd number of sts. Pick up same number for both bands.

Establish 1x1 ribbing (WS): (p^1, k1) to last st, p1

On non-buttonhole side, work as established in 1x1 ribbing for 1 (1, 1, 1.5, 1.5, 1.5, 1.5, **1.5, 1.5, 2, 2, 2, 2, 2**) inches, then bind off all sts knitwise on the RS.

On the buttohole side, work 2 (2,2,4,4,4,4,**4,4,6,6,6,6,6**) rows in 1x1 rib, work buttonhole row, work 3 (3,3,3,3,3,3,**3,3,5,5,5,5,5**) rows even in 1x1 rib, then bind off all sts knitwise on the RS.

Buttonholes: work 5 (5,5,5,5,5,5,**5,5,7,7,7,7,7**) buttonholes, evenly spaced in band *(or more or less as desired).*

To make a 3-stitch buttonhole in 1 row:
Slip next 2 sts. Pass the first st over the second (bind off), *sl 1, bind this st off* twice. Sl st from right needle onto left needle. Turn work and cast on 3 st knit wise.

If you find this buttonhole is too big or too small, you can work similar buttonholes by binding off then casting on 1, 2, or 4 sts in the same manner.

finishing: Using kitchener stitch graft the sleeve and body sts held at underarms and sew up any remaining gaps. Weave in all ends. Sew on buttons. Wet block your finished sweater, and enjoy!

irresistible earthy knits by Alexa Ludeman and Emily Wessel

antler hat

yummy toque in our favourite cable pattern  *by Alexa Ludeman*

If you are Canadian, you know what a toque is. And for you a toque is an essential accessory for winter, spring and fall too. While Vancouver lacks the sub-zero temperatures of Montreal and Halifax, it is cold, dreary and damp for a significant portion of the year. Is time for this year's new toque? Why not knit this classic, quick-knitting hat to match your antler cardigan!

sizing: Baby (Child, Adult S, L)
Head Circumference: 16 (18, 21, 23) inches

materials:

Yarn: 125 (150, 175, 200) yds worsted weight yarn
(we used Madelinetosh Vintage in 'twig')

Needles: US #4 / 4 mm and US # 5 / 8 mm
(or as required to meet gauge); 16" circular and/or double pointed needles

Gauge: 18 sts / 4"   *(in stockinette stitch)*

Notions: cable needle, stitch markers, darning needle

pattern: Using smaller needles CO 76 (84,96,110) sts, PM and join for working in the round. Work in 1x1 rib for 1.5 (2, 2, 2.5) inches. **For Adult S only:** work in 1x1 rib to last 2 sts, k2tog.

Change to larger needles and work set-up round:
[k16, p3(5,3,5)] around

Work antler cable pattern following chart or written instructions. Cable chart and instructions included in Antler Cardigan Pattern.

Round 1 (and all following odd rounds):
[work antler cable, p3(5,3,5)] around
Round 2 (and all following even rounds): work in pattern as established (knit the knits and purl the purls)

Work rows 1-6 of Antler Chart for a total of 5 (6, 8, 9) times, then proceed to decreases, switching to double pointed needles.

Decrease as follows:
Round 1:   (p1, p2tog, k4, c4b, c4f, k4) around
Round 2, 4, 6: work as established
Round 3:   (p2, k2, c4bd, k2tog, ssk, c4fd, k2) around
Round 5:   (p2tog, c4b, k4, c4f) around
Round 7:   (p1, k2tog, c4bd, c4fd, ssk)
Round 8:   (p1, k2tog 4 times) around
Round 9:   (p1, k2tog twice) around

Cut yarn leaving an 8 inch tail. Thread tail through remaining live stitches, pull tight and secure end. Weave in ends and enjoy!

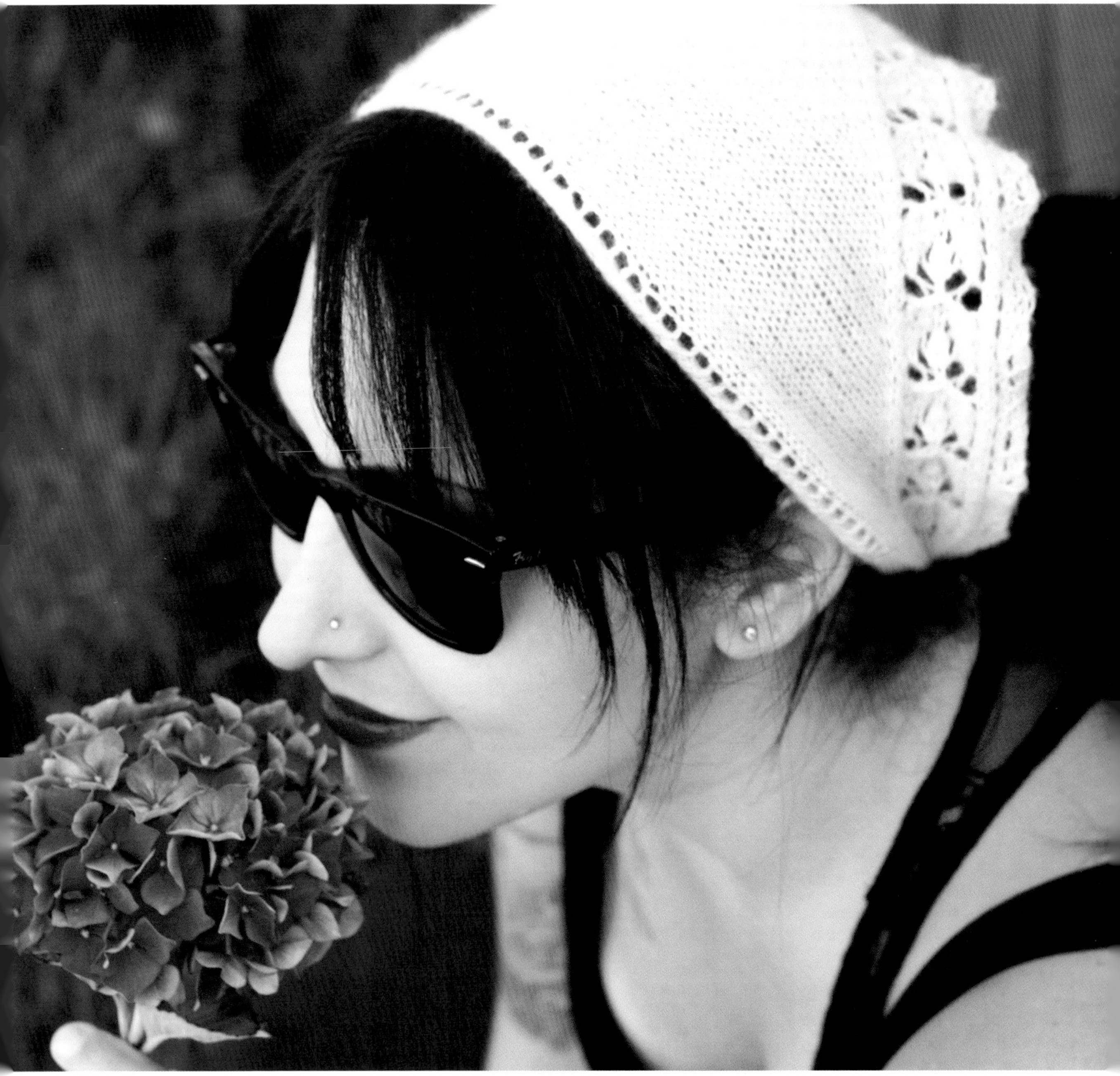

kits kerchief

girly lace kerchief for the modern domestic goddess  *by Emily Wessel*

I am a Kitsilano housewife; I sculpt my body at hot yoga, dine on organic food, and stroll down to the Granville Island Market for my weekly grocery-shop. I live the good life with my tall, dark, well-educated (and wealthy) husband. I have a busy volunteer schedule but still manage to find plenty of leisure time to bask in the sunshine at Kits beach and knit my heart out!   (ok... I must admit, this is a fantasy.. but an interesting fantasy nonetheless!)

This frothy little kerchief is the perfect addition to the hottie housewife's wardrobe. It also works for all the rest of us wannabes who still have to work for a living!

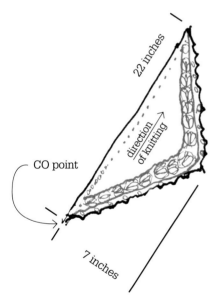

22 inches

direction of knitting

CO point

7 inches

sizing: Kerchief measures approximately 22 by 7 inches

The design is quite flexible and the finished fabric is quite stretchy. The finished size will depend on your gauge and how aggressively you block the kerchief.

The kerchief can also be made into a shawl. To do this, work [k4] instead of [sl3, p1] at the start of every WS row, and continue to increase until the shawl is 1/2 the desired length, working one even repeat, then decrease.

materials:

Yarn: 150 yds lace weight yarn for kerchief size
(sample shown in Plymouth Ecco Cashmere in 'natural')

Gauge: 26 sts / 4" in stockinette stitch

Needles: US #2 / 2.75 mm needles; straight or circular;
or as required to meet gauge

Notions: stitch markers, darning needle

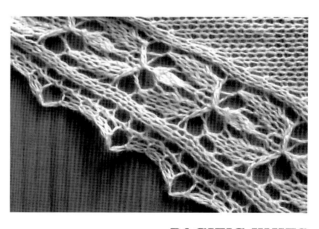

chart C - ending

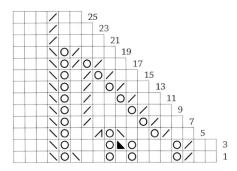

chart B - buttercup lace edge

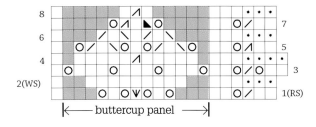

←———— buttercup panel ————→

chart A - setup

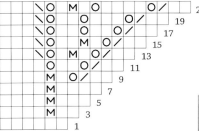

key & abbreviations

- ☐ **k** - knit on RS / purl on WS
- ⊡ **p** - purl on RS / knit on WS
- Ⓜ **m1** - make 1 stitch
- Ⓞ **yo** - yarn over
- Ⓥ **k1-yo-k1-tbl** - knit 1, yarn over, knit 1 through back loop (all in 1 stitch)
- ╱ **k2tog** - knit 2 together on RS / p2tog on WS
- ╲ **ssk** - slip, slip, knit on RS / p2tog-tbl on WS
- ⟋ **k3tog** - knit together on RS / p3tog on WS
- ◣ **sssk** - slip, slip, slip, k3tog through back loops on RS / p3tog-tbl on WS
- ▨ No Stitch

Chart Notes: Charts A and C show RS rows only; refer to text for WS instructions. Chart B shows both RS and WS rows; refer to key to determine how stitches are worked on RS vs. WS rows

pattern:

The kerchief is knit from end to end, increasing to the deepest point, then decreasing to the other end.

CO 6 sts. **First WS row:** sl3, p1, k2

Work rows 1-22 from chart A. RS rows are shown on chart. Work WS rows: sl3, purl to last 3 sts, k3

After chart A row 22 there are 17 sts.

Begin to work the body of the kerchief, including chart B. On the first row PM after working row 1 of of chart B to indicate the LH edge of the chart.

RS rows: work chart B, slip marker, k1, m1, knit to last 5 sts,
yo, ssk, k3   [1 st inc]
WS rows: sl3, purl to marker, work chart B to end

Work a total of 9 repeats of chart B.   [53 sts]

As you will notice, there are decreases on WS rows 4, 6, and 8 of the buttercup lace panel. The key indicates how these decreases are worked on the WS. For example, on row 4 there is a decrease; the key indicates that on the RS you would work k3tog, but on the WS you work p3tog.

Next work a single repeat of chart B without increasing:

RS rows: work chart B, knit to last 5 sts, yo, ssk, k3
WS rows: sl3, purl to marker, work chart B to end

After completing this 10th repeat of chart B there are 53 sts. Proceed to decrease as follows:

RS rows: work chart B, slip marker, ssk, knit to last 5 sts, yo,
                        ssk, k3   [1 st dec]
WS rows: sl3, purl to marker, work chart B to end

Work a total of 9 more repeats of chart B while decreasing. This is a total of 19 repeats worked in total.   [17 sts]

Work rows 1-25 from Chart C. RS rows are shown on chart. All WS rows as follows: sl3, purl to last 3 sts, k3

After chart C row 25 there are 6 sts.

Row 26:   sl3, p1, k2
Row 27 (bind-off): ssk, ssk, pass first st over second and off RH needle. Ssk once more, pass first st over second and off needles.

Break yarn, draw tail through last stitch and pull tight. Block kerchief aggressively to reveal the delicate lace pattern. Then tie it on and saunter down to your local farmer's market to get those heirloom tomatoes before they are all sold out!

low tide

sand and sea patterned cardigan *by Emily Wessel*

Low tide is a magical time of day. Creatures usually hidden below the waves become visible in tidal pools. The lace in this cardigan mimics the organic patterns left in the sand by the ebbing tide.

sizing: The pattern includes 5 child sizes and 7 adult sizes: 12 mo (2-3 yrs, 4-6 yrs, 7-9 yrs, 10-12 yrs, **adult S, M, L, XL, XXL, 3XL, 4XL**)

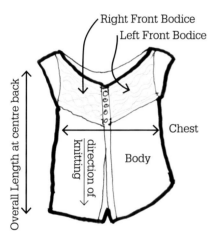

Size	Chest	Length	Yardage Required
12 mo	20"	12.5"	320
2-3 yrs	22"	14"	350
4-6 yrs	24"	14.5"	400
7-9 yrs	26"	16"	520
10-12 yrs	29"	17"	600
S	32"	18.5"	700
M	36"	19.5"	800
L	40"	20.5"	900
XL	44"	21.5"	1100
XXL	48"	22"	1200
3XL	52"	23"	1300
4XL	56"	24"	1400

materials:

Yarn: sock or 4-ply weight yarn: **refer to table for yardage** *(samples shown in Madelinetosh Tosh Sock in 'candlewick' and 'tern')*

Gauge: 24 sts / 4" in stockinette stitch

Needles: US #4 / 3.5mm and US #3 / 3.0 or 3.25mm needles; 24" or longer circular and double pointed needles for knitting sleeves in the round.

Notions: stitch markers, darning needle, C crochet hook, 4-7 buttons

pattern:

The cardigan is constructed as follows:
First the bodice pieces are knit: right and left fronts and back. Secondly stitches are picked up along the bottom of the bodice and the body is knit in one piece from bodice to hem. Lastly the sleeves are worked in the round.

chart A - 20 row repeat
right front and left back (right leaning bias)

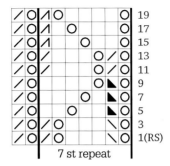

7 st repeat

Rows: 19, 17, 15, 13, 11, 9, 7, 5, 3, 1(RS)

chart B - 20 row repeat
left front and right back (left leaning bias)

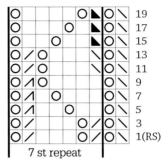

7 st repeat

Rows: 19, 17, 15, 13, 11, 9, 7, 5, 3, 1(RS)

Chart Notes: Charts illustrate RS (odd numbered) rows only. On WS rows, purl all sts. Refer to pattern instructions for edge sts worked either side of charts.

key & abbreviations

- **k** - knit
- **yo** - yarn over
- **k2tog** - knit two together
- **ssk** - slip, slip, knit
- **k3tog** - knit three together
- **sl1-k2tog-psso** - slip 1, k2tog, pass slipped st over

right front bodice:

Using smaller needles CO 24 (26,28,31,31,**31,33, 33,38,38,40,42**) sts. Knit 5 rows.

*The pattern is designed with crocheted button loops applied at the end (see instructions in **finishing** section). However, if you prefer you may work a number of evenly spaced buttonholes in the 3rd row of the initial garter band.*

Setup Row (WS): p4 (6,8,4,4,**4,6,6,4,4,6,8**), PM, purl to last 4 sts, k4

Switch to larger needles and work lace panel: *(for back left follow instructions from this point)*

RS rows: k4, work chart A to marker, knit
                 to end
WS rows: purl to last 4 sts, k4

Work a total of 30 (34,36,46,48,**52,54,56,62,64,64,70**) rows following chart A, ending with a WS row.

Work the next 2 rows 2 (2,2,0,1,**1,2,2,0,1,2,2**) times.

Next row: k4, yo, knit to marker, yo, knit to end
Next row: purl to last 4 sts, k4

There are 28 (30,32,31,33,**33,37,37,38,40,44,46**) sts on the needles. Put the first 4 sts on hold on one piece of waste yarn, and the remaining sts on hold on another piece. Break yarn, leaving 8" tail.

left front bodice:

Using smaller needles CO 24 (26,28,31,31,**31,33, 33,38,38,40,42**) sts. Knit 5 rows.

Next Row (WS): k4, purl to last 4 (6,8,4,4, **4,6,6,4,4,6,8**) sts, PM, purl to end

Switch to larger needles and work lace panel: *(for back right follow instructions from this point)*

RS rows: knit to marker, work chart B to last
                 4 sts, k4
WS rows: k4, purl to end

Work a total of 30 (34,36,46,48,**52,54,56,62,64,64,70**) rows following chart B, ending with a WS row.

Work the next 2 rows 2 (2,2,0,1,**1,2,2,0,1,2,2**) times.

Next row: knit to marker, yo, knit
                to last 4 sts, yo, k4
Next row: k4, purl to end

There are 28 (30,32,31,33,**33,37,37,38,40,44,46**) sts on the needles. Put the last 4 sts on hold on one piece of waste yarn, and the remaining sts on hold on another piece. Break yarn, leaving 8" tail.

back bodice:

The left half of the back bodice is worked first, then the CO sts are put back on needles and the right half of the back panel is worked.

CO 24 (26,28,31,31,**31,33,33,38,38,40,42**) sts using a provisional CO method and larger needles.

Setup Row (WS): p4 (6,8,4,4,**4,6,6,4,4,6,8**), PM, purl to last 4 sts, k4
Next row: knit
Next row: purl to last 4 sts, k4

Work lace panel following same instructions as for right front to end with same number of sts. Put sts on hold in the same manner. The left half of the back panel is now complete.

Place provisional CO sts back on larger needles. Ensure there are 24 (26,28,31,31,**31,33,33,38,38, 40,42**) sts. If not, increase to this total on first row.

Setup Row (WS): k4, purl to last 4 (6,8,4,4, **4,6,6,4,4,6,8**) sts, PM, purl to end
Next Row (RS):   knit
Next Row (WS):   k4, purl to end

Work lace panel following same instructions as for left front to end with same number of sts. Put sts on hold in the same manner. The back bodice is complete.

body:

Before working the body you must wet block the bodice pieces, pinning them out to approximately the size indicated on the schematic:

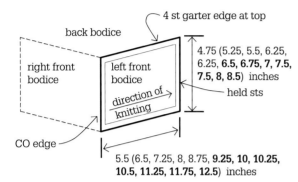

4 st garter edge at top

back bodice

right front bodice

left front bodice

direction of knitting

4.75 (5.25, 5.5, 6.25, 6.25, **6.5, 6.75, 7, 7.5, 7.5, 8, 8.5**) inches

held sts

CO edge

5.5 (6.5, 7.25, 8, 8.75, **9.25, 10, 10.25, 10.5, 11.25, 11.75, 12.5**) inches

Next work the shoulder seams. Making sure that wrong sides of bodice pieces are together, kitchener stitch the 4-st garter edge at the top of the R front to the 4-st garter edge at back, and do the same to attach L front to the back.

Next pick up sts along the edge of the bodice, and work in rows down to the hem. Using larger needles start at centre front and pick up 30 (33,36,39,42,**48,54,58,64,70,74,80**) sts, evenly spaced, along bottom edge of left front. CO 4 (4,5,5,8,**8,8,10,10,10,12,12**) sts at underarm. Pick up 60 (66,72,78,84,**96,108,116, 128,140,148,160**) sts, evenly spaced, along bottom edge of back. CO sts at second underarm as at first. Pick up sts along the bottom edge of the right front as at left front. [128 (140,154,166,184,**208,232,252, 276,300,320,344**) sts]

Setup row (WS): k4, p42(46,51,56,62,**70, 80,86,96,102,110,118**), PM, p36(40,44,46,52,**60, 64,72,76,88,92,100**), pm, purl to last 4 sts, k4

Work body as follows:

RS rows: k4, yo, knit to 2 sts before first marker, k2tog, slip marker, knit to second marker, slip marker, ssk, knit to last 4 sts, yo, k4
WS rows: k4, purl to last 4 sts, k4

Continue as established until body measures 8 (8.75, 9.25, 10, 11, **12, 13, 13.5, 14, 14.5, 15, 15.5**) inches from bottom edge of bodice to hem at centre back *(or desired length)*. Bind off all sts.

sleeves: work both the same

Put held sts from front and back bodice back on larger needles. With WS facing, beginning at sts CO at underarm, pick up 6 (6,6,8,8,**10,10,12,12,12,12,14**) sts, knit across held sts, pick up 2 sts in the side of the grafted neck edge, place marker for shoulder, pick up 2 more sts, knit across held sts, k3 (3,3,4,4,**5,5,6,6,6,7**), PM for start of round.
[58 (62,66,66,70,72,**80,82,84,88,96,102**) sts]

Knit 3 rounds, then proceed to short-row shaping.

short row shaping:

Knit to 9 (10,11,11,12,**12,13,14,14,15,16,17**) sts past shoulder marker, w&t (wrap and turn)

Purl to 9 (10,11,11,12,**12,13,14,14,15,16,17**) sts past shoulder marker, w&t

RS short row: knit to wrapped stitch. Work wrapped st by picking up wrap and knitting it together with the stitch it wraps. Then wrap the next stitch and turn work.

WS short row: purl to wrapped stitch, work wrapped stitch by picking up the wrap and working p2tog-tbl. Then wrap the next stitch and turn work.

Work last 2 rows a total of 9 (10,11,11,12,**12,13, 14,14,15,16,17**) times, then knit to end of round working wraps together with wrapped sts.

Knit 3 (3,4,4,5,5,**6,6,8,8,10,10**) rounds.
Bind off all sts.

finishing:

Button loops are worked in crochet on the right front. With WS facing, sc in first 2 rows, 3 ch, (skip 2 rows, 4 sc in next 4 rows, 3 ch) repeat 3 (3,3,4,4,**5,5,5,6,6,6,6**) times, then sc to end of right front bodice. Turn work.

With RS is facing, sl st to 3 ch loop, work 4 sc in each of the 3 ch loops, working sl st between loops.

Weave in ends, block garment and sew on buttons.

The lace panels and loose gauge of the stockinette stitch portion of this cardigan allow for the garment to be blocked considerably larger or left smaller as desired.

rosebud

foreign roses in a harsh landscape 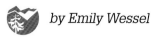 *by Emily Wessel*

Located on Canada's north-west coast, Desolation Sound is a wild and rugged place. Winter gales give way to brief summers, and the windswept landscape has little arable land. The European settlers on this remote coast did not let the elements stop them from carving out gardens to plant apples and roses.

These foreign seeds were coaxed to flower and fruit among the moss, ferns and native berries of the rain coast. Most of these remote homesteads have been abandoned and reclaimed by the wild, but in a forgotten garden you may still find a hardy rose entwined around an arbutus tree or sprawling untended in a sunny glade.

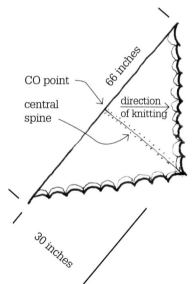

CO point

central spine

66 inches

direction of knitting

30 inches

sizing: The sample is knit in DK weight yarn, and measures 66 by 30 inches. Rosebud is also exquisite in sock or lace weight yarns, and you may work more or less pattern repeats to adjust the finished size. This particular lace stitch pattern looks best if it is knit at a fairly tight gauge (as far as lace goes).

materials:

Yarn: 700 yds DK, sock or lace weight yarn
(sample shown in SweetGeorgia Merino Silk Fine in 'china doll')

Gauge: 22 sts / 4" in stockinette stitch *(for DK weight yarn)*

Needles: US #4 / 3.5 mm *(or as required to meet gauge)*
32"+ circular needles

Notions: stitch markers, darning needle

irresistible earthy knits by Alexa Ludeman and Emily Wessel

chart C - edge - repeat rows 1-21 one time

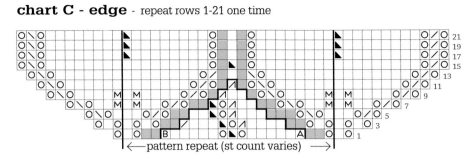

←—— pattern repeat (st count varies) ——→

chart B - rosebud lace pattern - repeat rows 1-24 four times (or more if desired)

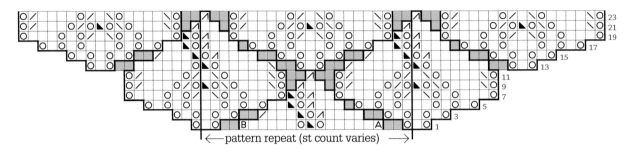

←—— pattern repeat (st count varies) ——→

Chart Notes: Charts represent RS rows only. Refer to text instructions for WS rows. Charts are worked from R to L, and from bottom to top.

chart A - setup - repeat rows 1-12 one time

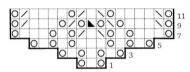

key & abbreviations

☐ **k** - knit

○ **yo** - yarn over

╱ **k2tog** - knit 2 together

╲ **ssk** - slip, slip, knit

╱ **k3tog** - knit 3 together

◣ **sssk** - slip, slip, slip, k3tog-tbl

▓ **No Stitch** (inserted for clarity of pattern)

Ⓐ work k1 on first repeat of each time chart is worked (at start of row and just after centreline stitch) then work ssk at all other repeats

Ⓑ work k2tog, **except** on last repeat of each time chart is worked work k1 (just before centreline and at end of row)

Ⓜ **m1** - make 1 stitch

pattern:

This shawl is knit from the centre top down to the scalloped edging, formed by two increasing triangles. The triangles are bounded by 3-st garter borders, and separated by a 1-st spine.

garter tab cast-on:

CO 3 sts provisionally. Knit 6 rows. Knit seventh row, pick up 3 sts along the border of the small garter stitch rectangle you have knit, then undo provisional cast on, put the 3 cast on sts on a needle, and knit them. [9 sts total]. *OR, if you prefer, simply CO 9 sts using any method desired.* Next work the first WS row: k3, p3, k3.

body of shawl:

Mark the fifth of the nine stitches. This stitch is the centreline stitch between the two lace panels.

The shawl is worked as described below, following charts A, B, and C in turn. Work the chart one time before the centreline, then a second time after the centreline (in both cases reading charts from R to L).

RS Rows: k3, work chart once, knit centreline st, work chart a second time, k3

WS Rows: k3, purl to last 3 sts, k3

Work rows 1-12 of chart A : setup   [41 sts]

Work rows 1-24 of chart B : rosebud lace 4 times   [329 sts]
For a larger shawl, work chart B more times (this will require more yarn)

Work rows 1-21 of chart C : edge   [413 sts]

Knit 1 row (WS), then bind off all sts on the RS using a stretchy bind off method. One that works well is: k1, (k1, place both sts back on LH needle, and k2tog-tbl) repeat to end. Cut yarn and pull through final stitch. Weave in ends, wet block your shawl, and enjoy!

all our love

hugs and kisses and gratitude from Alexa and Emily

Writing a book of any kind is a process. It takes time, dedication, and a lot of heart. We needed your love and support to get that done, thanks so much for being there.

We would like to thank our friends and families from the bottom of our hearts for listening to our dilemmas, posing for photos, cleaning the house (and tending the babe) while we knit feverishly!

Thanks to our models for bringing your beauty to our lives, and contributing it to this project. These regular fabulous folk (many of whom are related to Alexa) lent their time and faces to make our knits look fabulous. Thanks for posing and putting up with unreasonable cries of 'STOP BLINKING!'

The knits in this book could not have come about without our pattern testers. Thanks for taking the time to test our patterns and provide critiques and suggestions.

The knitting community has always been a source of inspiration and support for both of us. We would like to thank our local yarn shops and the dyers who have supported us. Felicia of SweetGeorgia yarns and Tanis of Tanis Fiber Arts have both trusted in our vision and supported us in working with their exquisite hand-dyed yarns. We love subtle hand dyes, and these two make the best we know!